Constitutional Change: A Critique of Dullea's "Charter Revision in the Empire State"

Sol Neil Corbin

Louis Lauer

American BookWorks Corporation

Library of Congress Card Number: 99-068215

ISBN: 1-884965-09-1

American BookWorks Corporation
309 Florida Hill Rd., Ridgefield, CT 06877

CONTENTS

Preface

1. Origin of the Commentaries Contained in this Book

Chapter 5 of Henrik N. Dullea's book, *Charter Revision in the Empire State: The Politics of New York's 1967 Convention*, published by The Rockefeller Institute Press in 1997, was called to our attention early this year. It discusses the New York Temporary State Commission on the Constitutional Convention (the "1966–1967 Commission") that prepared 15 substantive reports for the elected delegates to the 1967 Constitutional Convention in New York.

In purporting to attribute statements and actions to us as Commission Chairman and as Counsel to the 1966–1967 Commission, respectively, Chapter 5 greatly surprised us. Neither of us had ever been interviewed by Mr. Dullea concerning any aspect of the 1966–1967 Commission, its staff, its work product or its or our roles or objectives. Mr. Dullea's failure to seek out such obvious sources of highly relevant information for the purpose of verifying his inferences and conclusions is indefensible.[1]

As Commission Chairman and as Counsel to the 1966–1967 Commission, respectively, we know that Chapter 5 relies on baseless quotes and attributions and reaches unreliable and misleading conclusions about the work of the

1 An historian "is judged not simply by his veracity, but by his skill at verification." David Hackett Fischer, *Historians' Fallacies (Harper & Row, New York, 1970) at 40.*

1966–1967 Commission. For the convenience of the reader, Chapter 5's serious errors and misleading statements are described in our Summary that follows after this Preface and are more fully discussed in the two Commentaries that follow the Summary, one by Sol Neil Corbin and the other by Louis Lauer.

Cumulatively, our Commentaries demonstrate that Mr. Dullea's Chapter 5 is not based on appropriate scholarly research standards and does not adequately address basic issues of importance in planning for future constitutional conventions in New York State. We therefore deemed it essential to set the record straight.

2. Our Initial Efforts to Set the Record Straight

At first our Commentaries had a limited purpose: to correct the biased and erroneous discussion of the 1966–1967 Commission in Mr. Dullea's book, *Charter Revision in the Empire State: The Politics of New York's 1997 Constitutional Convention* (the "Dullea Book" or "Charter Revision"). Published in 1997 by The Rockefeller Institute Press, the Dullea Book is a revised version of Mr. Dullea's Ph.D. dissertation completed in 1982. In our opinion, as demonstrated in our Commentaries, Chapter 5 of the Dullea Book is flawed by Dullea's failures to follow rudimentary research procedures and by partisan preconceptions that impaired any objective analysis of the Commission's members, its staff, its 75 consultants, and their combined work product.

As the draft of our Commentaries was completed, we took a next step. Because the Dullea Book had been endorsed as a scholarly work by Richard P. Nathan, the Director of The Nelson A. Rockefeller Institute of Government, we thought it important for The Rockefeller Institute to publish and distribute our corrective essays to those the Institute knew had acquired the Dullea Book. After all, The Rockefeller Institute describes itself as the public policy institute of the State University of New York. As a public institution it has a special obligation to inform and not mislead scholars — an obligation that gave special significance to its Director's mistaken endorsement of the Dullea Book. In our view, The Institute therefore was obligated to take corrective action to bring those facts to the attention of those who had been — and to future scholars who might be — misled by Chapter 5 of the Dullea Book.

Moreover, we were concerned that the Institute needed to take corrective action to dispel the substantial risk that the errors and distortions contained in the Dullea Book would be perpetuated and spread. This risk is especially high because of the customary research practice of accepting and building on the seemingly scholarly publications of others.

3. Correspondence with The Rockefeller Institute

On April 6, 1999, Sol Corbin sent a letter and two typewritten copies of our Commentaries to Dr. Richard P. Nathan, Director of The Rockefeller Institute, who had written the foreword to the Dullea book. One copy of our Commentaries was for Dr. Nathan, who had endorsed the scholarly quality of Mr. Dullea's work and thereby lent to it the Institute's reputation for accurate and disinterested scholarship; the other copy was for forwarding to Mr. Dullea, to afford him an opportunity to correct his erroneous and misleading presentation. The letter (a copy which is set forth at pp. 29–31 of this Preface) strongly urged Dr. Nathan as Director of The Rockefeller Institute (part of the State

University of New York) to publish the Commentaries "and see that they are also distributed to prior and future recipients of Mr. Dullea's book."

In response, Mr. Corbin received a letter dated May 12, 1999 from Michael Cooper, Director of The Rockefeller Institute Press, rejecting the request that the Commentaries be published and distributed by The Rockefeller Institute Press. Without referring to Dr. Nathan's endorsement of the scholarly quality of the Dullea book, Mr. Cooper, while acknowledging that the Commentaries provided a "very good basis for debate," asserted that it was "not the role of the publisher to moderate such debate."

Mr. Corbin also received in May 1999 a copy of a letter dated May 2, 1999 sent by Mr. Dullea to Dr. Nathan, defending what Mr. Dullea referred to as the "book version" of his Ph.D. dissertation. He stated in that letter that his "dissertation" was based on interviews, but that he no longer had the notes of those interviews. He also acknowledged that he had never communicated with either of us before he wrote his dissertation or authorized its publication in "book version". He did assert, however, that even if he had, "I do not think that I would have modified much of what I said concerning their conflicts" with the first Executive Director of the 1966–1967 Commission, nor would he have "significantly changed [his] report of how the delegates to the Convention felt about the 1966–1967 Commission's work."

Not satisfied with the Cooper and Dullea responses to his April 6, 1999 letter to Dr. Nathan, Mr. Corbin wrote Dr. Nathan on June 2, 1999, again urging him to "undertake for the Institute to print and distribute our Commentaries." (A copy of this letter is set forth at pp. 32–33 of this Preface.)

To enable scholars to assess for themselves the merits of Mr. Cooper's and Mr. Dullea's letters, Mr. Corbin's June 2, 1999 letter also asked Dr. Nathan that if he rejected the request, he obtain "for us Mr. Cooper's and Mr. Dullea's authorization to publish as part of our Commentaries their May letters responding to our Commentaries."

Dr. Nathan responded by letter dated June 17, 1999, stating that he has "no objection to [our] distributing a copy of [his] letter." (A copy of Dr. Nathan's letter is set forth at pp. 34–35 of this Preface.) Instead of obtaining Mr. Dullea's authorization to publish Mr. Dullea's May 2, 1999 letter to him, the letter advises Corbin to communicate directly with Dullea "as to whether he would give [Corbin] permission to publish his letter." (The letter is silent on Corbin's request that he obtain Mr. Cooper's authorization to publish his May 12, 1999 letter.) As for the renewed request that The Rockefeller Institute publish our Commentaries, Dr. Nathan wrote:

> "It is our position — and this is customary for publishers — that it is not our appropriate role to print and disseminate commentaries on books and other publications we issue."

Had Dr. Nathan, in his capacity as Director of The Rockefeller Institute, refrained from endorsing the scholarly quality of the Dullea Book, we would not question his statement that publishers "customarily" do not print and disseminate commentaries on books and other publications they issue. Here, however, by endorsing the Dullea Book in the foreword signed by him as Director of the Institute itself, he lent the Institute's reputation to a flawed and poorly researched discussion of the work of the 1966–1967 Commission. Therefore, as it is the Institute's obligation to inform and not mislead future scholars, it should have corrected its failure by the publication and distribution of our Commentaries.

As Dr. Nathan would not undertake that corrective action, we now do so to enable scholars and others interested in constitutional change to make an informed judgment about the work of the 1966–1967 Commission — and an independent judgment, based on documentary evidence, as to the propriety of the Institute's refusal to do so itself.

4. Subsequent Developments

After The Rockefeller Institute rejected for the second time our request that it print and circulate our Commentaries to those who had acquired the Dullea Book, we perused the balance of the Dullea Book. We then looked at what Dr. Richard P. Nathan referred to as a "companion volume" — *Decision 1997: Constitutional Change in New York* ("Decision 1997") — a book of essays also published in 1997 by The Rockefeller Institute Press. Finally, we read the 1995 Final Report of the 1993-95 Temporary New York State Commission on Constitutional Revision (the "1995 Commission Final Report"), Peter C. Goldmark, Jr., Chairman, appointed by Governor Mario Cuomo. (As Dr. Nathan stated in a foreword to Decision 1997, the "material" presented in that volume "grew out of the work" of the Commission on Constitutional Revision appointed in 1993 by Governor Cuomo.)

The combination of the two books published by The Rockefeller Institute Press and the 1995 Final Report of the Cuomo-appointed 1993–1995 Commission led us to go beyond our original limited purpose of correcting the errors and misleading statements contained in the Dullea Book's

Chapter 5 discussion of the 1966–1967 Commission. We then expanded on our Commentaries to a more general discussion of constitutional conventions for possible future use by scholars. This general discussion involves (1) our discovery that prominent scholars had relied on the misleading characterization of the Commission in Chapter 5 of the Dullea Book; (2) the proper orientation of New York commissions formed to prepare for constitutional conventions; and (3) the most appropriate form for submitting to New York's voters the constitutional changes proposed by a constitutional convention.

A. *Mistaken Reliance by Scholars on the Dullea Book*

The significance of the Institute's failure to take corrective action is illustrated in Decision 1997, the companion book to the Dullea Book. Decision 1997 shows how scholars, acting in good faith in their own work, mistakenly relied on the Dullea Book, thus inadvertently spreading the errors in the Dullea Book promoted by The Rockefeller Institute.

The evidence of that reliance is contained in a thoughtful essay in Decision 1997, titled "The Role of the Constitutional Commission in State Constitutional Change," by Robert F. Williams, Distinguished Professor of Law at Rutgers University School of Laws in Camden, New Jersey. Alluding to Professor Peter J. Galie's "The New York Constitution: A Reference Guide" (Greenwood Press, 1991) (the "Reference Guide"), an independent publication, Professor Williams in his essay writes as follows about the 1966–1967 Commission:

> "After the New York voters approved the call of a constitutional convention in 1965, the legislature

> created a Temporary Commission on the Constitutional Convention. Galie reports that this commission was 'plagued by partisan divisions,' and had little impact on the Convention." (Decision 1997, at p. 50)

As support for this statement, Professor Williams, in his footnote 23, cites pages 28-29 of Professor Galie's 1991 Reference Guide.

Reflecting on the fact that Professor Galie's cited work had been published in 1991 — a quarter of a century after the 1966–1967 Commission did its work — Lauer intuited that "Galie's report" had not been based on Galie's personal observation or independent research. Lauer also surmised that Professor Galie, following a common scholarly practice, had based his "report" on what he had unwittingly assumed was an objective, scholarly treatise by Mr. Dullea.

To verify surmise with actual fact, Lauer determined to interview Professor Galie about the "report." He accordingly called Professor Galie, Professor of Political Science at Canisius College, in Buffalo, New York on August 31, 1999 to ascertain the factual basis for Professor Galie's 1991 report in his "Reference Guide" that the 1966–1967 Commission was "plagued by partisan divisions."

At the outset of that conversation, Lauer told Professor Galie that he had been Counsel to the 1966–1967 Commission from its early days until its work was done. Lauer then read to Professor Galie Professor Williams' quotation from Professor Galie's "Reference Guide" that the Commission was "plagued by partisan divisions" and asked Professor Galie for the basis of that remark.

Professor Galie promptly responded that his 1991 report in his "Reference Guide" had not been based on any independent factual research, but had been based on secondary sources. He continued that his principal — and possibly his only — source had been a 1982 Ph.D. dissertation by Henrik Dullea (a revised version of which is the Dullea Book).

On September 1, 1999, Lauer called Professor Williams at Rutgers University Law School at Camden, New Jersey, to advise him that Professor Galie's "report" on which he had relied had not been based on Galie's personal observation or independent research, but at least principally on Dullea's 1982 Ph.D. dissertation. This was news to Professor Williams who again confirmed, as his citation indicated, that in characterizing the Commission, he had relied in his 1997 essay only on Professor Galie's 1991 report.

We do not know which scholars in addition to Professors Galie and Williams, following customary procedures of building on the seemingly scholarly reports of others, have relied on the Dullea Ph.D. dissertation or its revised version published as the Dullea Book by The Rockefeller Institute Press and endorsed by Dr. Nathan. Based on what we have learned from reading Professor Williams' essay in Decision 1997 since the June 1999 exchange of correspondence between Mr. Corbin and Dr. Nathan, we were more persuaded than ever that it is necessary to correct Dullea's erroneous and misleading discussion of the 1966–1967 Commission.

B. *Proper Orientation of Future New York Preparatory Commissions*

As discussed in detail in our Commentaries, a major issue treated in the Dullea Book concerns whether the

1966-67 Commission should have made substantive policy recommendations to the elected delegates to the Convention. The Commission *unanimously* decided, after public hearings and due consideration, that it should not make such substantive policy recommendations. Instead, it *unanimously* decided to prepare objective briefing papers that defined constitutional issues, presented alternative approaches to those issues and examined the arguments for and against each alternative — leaving it to the elected delegates to make the substantive policy decisions. In his Book, Mr. Dullea stressed those who, he alleged, took issue with that unanimous decision.

How should future New York preparatory commissions orient their work? This question is put in perspective by Chairman Peter C. Goldmark, Jr.'s February 1995 letter transmitting to Governor George E. Pataki, Senate Majority Leader Joseph L. Bruno, Assembly Speaker Sheldon Silver and other members of the State Legislature the 1995 Final Report of the 1993–1995 Commission. (All of the members of that Commission, *including* Mr. Dullea and Dr. Nathan, had been appointed by Governor Mario Cuomo in May 1993 in advance of a future vote in 1997 on whether a convention should be held in 1999.) The Goldmark letter explained:

> "Unlike its predecessors, this [1993–1995] Commission was not created to prepare materials to inform the work of constitutional convention delegates for a convention certain to be held. We decided therefore to cast our net broadly, seeking to learn from New Yorkers their views about both the condition of their government and the prospect of a con-

> stitutional convention to deal with the problems they identified as most pressing."

Chairman Goldmark's letter continued that based on the 1993-95 Commission's work, a "large majority" of that commission had identified "four key areas of government" in which, they believed, "the State has persistently fallen short of achieving serious and far reaching reform." That majority, including Mr. Dullea and Dr. Nathan, then recommended that the Governor and Legislature establish Action Panels "to break the gridlock in those areas." Chairman Goldmark's letter then reported:

> "The success of the Action Panels, a large majority of the Commission concludes, would preclude the need for a constitutional convention. Without immediate and decisive action to achieve wide-ranging reform, however, the majority recommends support for a convention."

Mr. Goldmark returned to this theme in his Introduction to Decision 1997 (co-edited by Mr. Dullea). In that Introduction, Mr. Goldmark remarked (at page xvi) that the 1993-95 Commission "was appointed by Governor Cuomo in May 1993 to help voters prepare for the vote they will cast in 1997" on whether to hold a constitutional convention. As the recommended Action Panels had not been formed by the time he wrote his Introduction to Decision 1997, Mr. Goldmark writes (at page xix) that "as one New Yorker who cares about good government and restoring the greatness of our state, I find the case for a constitutional convention increasingly compelling." (A majority of the voters, voting in November 1997 against the calling of a constitutional convention, apparently reached the opposite conclusion.)

Looking to the future, it is possible that a statute enacted by the Legislature and approved by the Governor will direct a preparatory commission (1) to make a comprehensive review of the Constitution, *and* (2) to make substantive policy recommendations for constitutional revision or amendment to the elcted convention delegates. (Such recommendations may be to retain, modify, or delete one or more existing provisions, or incorporate one or more new provisions.) Upon such a direction by the Legislature and Governor, a preparatory commission, of course, would be obligated to make such recommendations.

In the absence of such an express direction, however, the lessons described by Mr. Goldmark's 1995 letter and his Introduction to Decision 1997 suggest that the following rules should be followed in defining the proper orientation of future preparatory constitutional commissions appointed by both the Governor and the Legislature:

> 1. If such a commission is formed *before* the voters have decided to have a constitutional convention and if the clear purpose of the commission is to assist the voters decide *whether to hold a convention*, it would be proper for the commission to make recommendations bearing on the question whether such a convention should be held. (This course was followed by the 1993-95 Commission formed by Governor Cuomo and chaired by Mr. Goldmark.)
>
> 2. If such a commission is formed *after* the voters have decided to have a constitutional convention and if the clear purpose of the commission is to assist the

elected convention delegates perform their function of proposing to the voters a revised constitution or amendments to the constitution, it would be proper for the commission to prepare briefing papers, without endorsement of any substantive policy recommendations. (This course was followed by the 1966-67 Commission appointed by the Governor and Legislative Leaders after the voters had voted in 1965 for a constitutional convention to be held in 1967.)

C. *Submission of Proposed Changes to the Voters*

Under the New York State Constitution, the product of a constitutional convention, before taking effect, is required to be submitted to the voters for their approval on referendum. The proposed changes may be grouped together in one proposed new constitution or may be contained in separate propositions, each of which is voted on separately.

The question, then, is how should future constitutional conventions submit their proposed changes to the voters? The 1967 Convention chose to submit its proposed changes to the voters in what has been referred to as "a single package" — a new constitution, presenting the voters with an all-or-nothing decision. In doing so, it departed from the precedent set by the prior constitutional convention, the 1938 Convention, which grouped its recommendations in nine separate propositions, six of which were approved and three of which were rejected by the voters. In contrast to the 1938 Convention's product, the single package submitted by the 1967 Convention was rejected, according to Dullea, by the voters "in every county of the state." He further reports that the "final vote was 3,487,513 against; 1,327,999 in favor," or an overwhelming margin of almost 3 to 1. (Dullea, "Constitutional Revision in 1967: Learning the Right Lessons from the Magnificent Failure," at pp. 379-80 of Decision 1997.)

What then is the "right lesson" to be learned from the contrasting results of the 1938 and the 1967 New York Constitutional Conventions?

The obvious general lesson (which, as described in Lauer's Commentary, he applied in his work for the 1968-70 Suffolk County Charter Revision Commission) is that a New York constitutional convention should group its proposed changes in separate propositions that enable the voters to choose what they favor and what they disfavor. By respecting the voters' prerogatives, that course increases the likelihood that the voters will have confidence in the convention and therefore approve at least some of its product. (As elaborated in Lauer's Commentary, by applying that lesson, the Suffolk County Charter Revision Commission earned the Suffolk County voters' trust and confidence, and they approved *all* of that Commission's proposals.)

This obvious lesson is not drawn by Dullea either in the Dullea Book or in his 1997 essay, "Constitutional Revision in 1967: Learning the Right Lesson from the Magnificent Failure" in Decision 1997. Indeed, Dullea seems preoccupied with proving that the 1967 Convention, whose work product was rejected by almost a 3 to 1 statewide margin and in every county of the state both within and outside New York City, was a "magnificent failure." He does not even analyze whether New York's 1938 and 1967 experiences with constitutional conventions permit a compelling general rule: as in 1967, the voters reject all-or-nothing state constitutional submissions, but, as in 1938, selectively approve or disapprove separate state constitutional propositions.

This curious omission in what purports to be scholarly work also impelled us beyond the original limited purpose of our Commentaries. As a result, we next discuss (1) the arguments advanced by Dullea in support of his assertion that the 1967 Convention was a "magnificent failure," and (2) the reasons we conclude that it was "a readily foreseeable failure" that deservedly followed the Convention's disregard for strongly expressed public opinion.

A convenient starting point is Dullea's own statement in appraising various descriptions of the 1967 experience: "Taking our cue from former Governor Al Smith, that great genius of New York State's political history, 'Let's look at the record.'" (Decision 1997, at p. 369)

According to Dullea's account in the Dullea Book (at p. 325) of the final debate of the 1967 Convention on September 26, the Convention's Committee on Presentation then proposed the adoption by the delegates of a resolution calling for the "single submission" of the Convention's work product in one new constitution. Dullea continues that in support, "Congressman Keogh [Committee Chairman] posed the fundamental question of the day" by stating:

> The pending resolution "imposes upon the people, the sovereign people of the State of New York, only one, simple, direct, understandable question: 'Do you want what we have done or do you not?'"

Dullea then reports that in response, Judge Harry Goldman, Committee Vice-Chairman, "went on to quote another famous Democrat at the 1938 Convention, Governor Alfred E. Smith," identified by Dullea in his essay contained in Decision 1997 as "that great genius of New York State politics," as follows:

> "If you do not give the people a chance to speak separately, they will place the Constitution on the block and chop its head off."[2]

In insisting that the 1967 Convention submit its product to the voters in one all-or-nothing package, the Convention, of course, denied "the people a chance to speak separately." As Governor Smith's maxim anticipated, the voters then placed the proposed Constitution "on the block and chopped its head off" by rejecting the proposal by almost a 3 to 1 margin.

Even more dramatic confirmation of Governor Smith's maxim is provided by the following data presented by Dullea:

---

2 Dullea (Charter Revision, pp. 322-23) also notes that in Governor Nelson A. Rockefeller's final Special Message to the 1967 Convention, he urged the delegates not to present the voters with a "take it or leave it decision." In support of that advice, he quoted the following remarks at the 1938 Convention of Senator Robert F. Wagner, father of Mayor Robert F. Wagner, Jr., Vice Chairman of the 1967 Convention (and a member of the 1966-67 Constitutional Convention Commission):

> "Until a few days ago it was generally accepted in this Convention that the proposals picked out by the Committee are proposals that ought to be submitted separately. ... If you combine them all together you are going to invite the opposition to all the proposals as one army against the entire Constitution."

Interestingly, Governor Rockefeller did not join that "army." Instead, according to Dullea, the Governor formally made known that he "would personally vote for the Constitution, but he urged the state's voters to make their own decision." (Charter Revision, p. 337)

"Despite its position as the last of four referenda on the ballot, approximately 14,000 more votes were cast on the constitutional question than on the $2.5 billion transportation bond issue, which led the ballot and was approved by a margin of over 790,000. *The voters obviously searched out the proposed Constitution on the ballot to make sure their voices would be heard.*" (Charter Revision, p. 341; emphasis supplied)

"More than 1.5 million additional voters cast their ballot in the 1967 ratification campaign than in the 1965 call of the Convention. *In an off-year election, they went out of their way to come to the polls and vote against the proposed charter.*" (Charter Revision, p. 390; emphasis supplied.)

In view of these facts, Dullea could not — and does not — dispute that the 1967 Convention was a "failure" in the sense that it overwhelmingly failed to have its proposed constitution approved by the people on whose behalf the Convention was created. This indisputable conclusion, when mixed with what obviously is Dullea's strong sympathy for the Democratic leadership at the 1967 Convention, seems to have led him to conclude the Dullea Book with Chapter 16, titled "A Magnificent Failure?" — which answered in the affirmative the question he posed in the title of Chapter 16 about the 1967 Convention.

D. *Dullea's Arguments that the 1967 Convention's Failure was "Magnificent"*

To enable disinterested scholars to judge for themselves the nature of the 1967 Convention's failure, we now review the arguments advanced by Dullea in support of his conclusion that the failure was "magnificent".

(1) *A claimed mandate in electing delegates.* Dullea argues that the "comfortable majority [of convention delegates] gained by the Democrats [in the election of delegates] was more than sufficient reason for the party's leadership to later claim that it had been given a mandate to produce a new and substantially shortened constitution." (Charter Revision, p. 379) This "mandate" presumably required — or at least justified — the Democratic Party's leadership's decision to submit in a single package on an all-or-nothing basis what Dullea describes as the Convention's 38 proposed changes.

Does the factual record presented by Dullea himself support his argument that there "was more than sufficient reason for the party's leadership to later claim that it had been given a mandate to produce a new and substantially shortened constitution"? Or does it, on the contrary, prove that the delegates did not have any specific mandate to justify their action?

The following factual account by Dullea himself makes his argument about a "claimed mandate" seem like the "spin" of a political loyalist, rather than the reasoned analysis of a disciplined scholar:

> "Neither primary nor general-election campaigns were substantially related to prospective Convention issues. Even the efforts of the Catholic Church to obtain advance commitments with respect to repeal of the Blaine Amendment [which was believed more restrictive than the Federal Constitu-

> tion's First Amendment on church-state relations] failed to produce clear examples of electoral campaigns centered on this issue. *To the extent that delegates looked to voters for instructions on a broad array of constitutional issues, they were invariably disappointed.*" (Charter Revision, p. 378; emphasis added.)

Moreover, in his essay in Decision 1997, Dullea presents data that go beyond the quoted generalization concerning the absence of instructions on "a broad array of constitutional issues" and evidences the absence of a mandate on the specific issue of "a new and substantially shortened constitution." Thus, he writes (Essay, in Decision 1997, p. 373):

> "The 'frequency of amendment, cumbersome document' issue was mentioned by only one delegate in my interview cohort, hardly indicative of a broad-based mandate for fundamental constitutional reform."

In short, the specific factual information that led Dullea to conclude it was "hardly indicative of a broad-based mandate for fundamental constitutional reform" flatly contradicts his argument that there was "more than sufficient reason" for claims of "a mandate to produce a new and substantially shortened constitution."

(2) *The Subsequent Adoption of Convention Ideas*. We infer from Dullea's discussion of what he calls "The Legacy of the Convention" (Charter Revision, pp. 390-97) that, in his judgment, the "success" or "failure" of a constitutional convention should not be measured solely by the results of the referendum on the convention's work product. He there writes that "in the thirty years since the 1967 Convention,

twenty-two of its thirty-eight proposed amendments were adopted." He continues (at p. 390):

> "The incorporation into state policy of new ideas contained in the 1967 draft has been substantial, although much of this activity has been statutory rather than constitutional."

We agree that the impact of a constitutional convention over time should be taken into account when making a full assessment of its "success" or "failure" in discharging its responsibility to review existing constitutional provisions and propose appropriate changes, if any, for voter approval. To the extent, however, that in the case of the 1967 Convention, the impact "has been statutory rather than constitutional," it puts into question the claim that the Convention produced a short, simplified constitution that dispensed with "legislative detail". Moreover, statutory changes do not have the same "impact": unlike constitutional changes, they may be changed at will by the Legislature and the Governor, without voter approval.

To the extent that the impact of the 1967 Convention was through constitutional amendments adopted by the voters over a period of thirty years, it underlines the magnitude of the failure produced by the Convention's decision to combine its 38 proposals in one proposition on an all-or-nothing basis. If the 1967 Convention had recognized the force of Governor Smith's maxim and followed the precedent set by the 1938 Convention (six of whose nine propositions were adopted), those changes might have been approved in 1967, effective January 1, 1968, rather than over a period of 30 years.

(3) *Propositions "woven together" in one document.* Mr. Dullea recognizes that the 1967 Convention's decision to submit its 38 proposals in one basic document on an all-or-nothing basis bears profoundly on any assessment of the success or failure of the Convention. He discusses this decision both in his Charter Revision book and in his 1997 essay, "Constitutional Revision in 1967: Learning the Right Lessons from the Magnificent Failure" in Decision 1997. Here is his focused summary in his 1997 essay in Decision 1997:

> "Why were not such issues as Blaine [relating to church-state relations] and the debt referendum [requiring a referendum for the incurrence of state debt] stripped out of the basic document and submitted separately to the people for determination? Some have argued that the reason was Travia's [the Convention President's] commitment to the Catholic hierarchy that he would give them the best hope of the repeal of Blaine by burying it in the entire document. I would disagree. He and other members of the convention's leadership recognized the political difficulties associated with their determination, and even the Church's leadership ultimately took pains not to be associated with the all-or-nothing approach.
>
> "Rather, those in command of the convention concluded that they had done what they sought to do. They had come together for six months and debated an extraordinary litany of issues, from wiretaps and eavesdropping devices to relations between church and state, many of which would have received only fleeting consideration in the day-to-day operations of the state legislature. Their product was

not a consensus document, but it was one that had been forged in the crucible of sharply divided partisan debate. *It was a new document, not a series of piecemeal amendments to the charter of 1894. Its articles were woven together into a coherent whole.* While its provisions might not appeal to one and all, it deserved to be judged, they thought, as a whole on its merits." ("Learning the Right Lessons from the Magnificent Failure", Decision 1997 at p. 379; emphasis supplied.)

Dullea's attempted justification for the decision to submit 38 proposals in one document for voter approval on an all-or-nothing basis thus amounts to an argument that the proposals "were woven together into a coherent whole" and therefore the "new document" deserved to be judged "as a whole on its merits." But the very issues he mentions in the long quotation (above) of his argument prove that the 1967 Convention's proposals, like those of the 1938 Convention, were *not* "woven together into a coherent whole" and could have been grouped in separate propositions.

For example, in the 1894 Constitution, there was not any "weaving together" of the Blaine Amendment on church-state relations and the requirement of a referendum for the incurrence of state debt, although both provisions appear in that document. Nor does Dullea present a single reason for concluding that these distinct issues have any necessary connection in the philosophic or practical operations of government. Absent such a connection, either one could have been repealed while the other was retained. Indeed, Dullea proves the point in his report that some groups who strongly favored change in the referendum requirement for the incurrence of state debt even more strongly opposed repeal of the Blaine Amendment, while others who strongly favored repeal of the Blaine Amendment even more strongly opposed change in the existing referendum requirement.

Here is a wide range of three other examples drawn from Dullea's discussion of "The Legacy of the Convention" that make clear that not all of the 38 proposals of the 1967 Convention were "woven together" in such a way that the Convention could not have properly grouped them in separate propositions for voters' consideration and approval:

(a) Proposed "restrictions on the use of wiretapping and electronic surveillance" went down to defeat as part of the rejected single package, but were later adopted by legislation (Charter Revision, pp. 391-2). Those restrictions certainly were not "woven together" with proposals concerning church-state relations, a referendum requirement for the incurrence of state debt or state assumption of the costs of social welfare.

(b) The Convention's proposal to change the base for legislative apportionment from citizen population to total population also went down to defeat in 1967 as part of the rejected single package, but was adopted in a separate constitutional amendment submitted to the people in 1969 (Charter Revision, p. 392). Any opposition to that amendment on the ground that it could not be properly adopted without the simultaneous adoption of other constitutional amendments on church-state relations, state debt incurrence and state assumption of the costs of social welfare obviously would have been viewed as rank sophistry and rejected out of hand.

(c) According to Dullea,

> "The most 'successful' section of the proposed Constitution may well have been Arthur Levitt, Jr.'s, 'Conservation Bill of Rights.' Passed verbatim by two successive Legislatures immediately after the 1967 defeat, this fundamental commitment to the protection of the state's environment was approved by the voters in 1969" (Charter Revision, pp. 394-5).

Nothing — absolutely nothing — in Dullea's treatment of that development suggests that a "Conservation Bill of Rights" was so "woven together" with other provisions of the single package submitted by the 1967 Convention that it could not properly have been presented to the voters as a separate proposition in 1967 and been adopted two years earlier than it ultimately was.

In short, despite its surface glitter, the argument that the 1967 Convention had to submit all of its proposals to the voters in one package on an all-or-nothing basis because all of its proposals were "woven together" in one document is completely without merit. Under the circumstances, it is not plausible to assert, as Dullea does, that the Democratic leadership of the 1967 Convention insisted on the submission of a single package on an all-or-nothing basis because the Convention's 38 proposals were "woven together." It is more plausible to assume that, as is permissible under the New York constitutional provisions governing the work of constitutional conventions, the Convention's leadership grouped unrelated proposals together in the hope that the voters would be compelled to accept those they did not like in order to get those they favored.

(4) *1967 Convention accomplishments.* In the concluding paragraph of his Charter Revision (at pp. 403-4), Dullea

pays tribute to the Democratic Party leadership and states forcefully his justification for describing as a "magnificent failure" a Convention whose work product the voters rejected by a margin of almost 3 to 1. Here is the entire concluding paragraph:

> "Travia [Convention President] had forged a draft Constitution out of inter-party and intra-party conflict, and he was willing to put that document to the test of voter approval. But he and his Democratic colleagues seriously misunderstood the depth and breath of sentiment on the church-state issue, and the specificity (and scope) of their policy objectives gave the Republicans a barn door-size target of fiscal irresponsibility at which to aim their opposition campaign. Yet, they had run a scandal-free Convention, hired a professionally respected staff, grappled with most of the major issues, prevented further incursions on the Constitution by pressure groups other than the Church, and finished their deliberations on time. They had aggregated a host of complex constitutional issues into a single choice for the electorate, but unlike the vote on a candidate for political office, who is able to mediate and take advantage of conflicting pressures to the fullest, the single-package alternative aggravated policy concerns and resulted in the accumulation of negative responses. The end result was the same in New York as in Maryland: a magnificent failure."

By what standard may it be said, based on Dullea's presentation in the final paragraph of his book, that the 1967 Convention's failure was "characterized by greatness of achievement" (an apposite definition from the Oxford Dictionary definition of "magnificent")? On analysis, it is obvious that the quoted paragraph contains the following items that negate greatness of achievement: (a) the Democratic leadership "seriously misunderstood the depth and breadth of sentiment on the church-state issue" (in plainer language, the Democratic leadership underestimated the opposition to repeal of the Blaine Amendment); and (b) the "specificity (and scope) of their policy objectives" made them vulnerable to a charge of "fiscal irresponsibility" (that is, the community development, urban education and social services proposals suggested, as Dullea put it in his 1997 essay, "the possibility of future massive tax increases ... to be accomplished in part by removing the requirement for voter approval of all general obligation state debt.") (Decision 1997, p. 379). Some might add to the negative side of the balance sheet Dullea's statement that the Democratic leadership "aggregated a host of complex constitutional issues into a single choice ... that aggravated policy concerns and resulted in an accumulation of negative responses."

In contrast to the negative items that contributed to the failure of the Convention to have its work product approved by the voters, Dullea notes on the positive side that: (a) the Convention was scandal-free; (b) the Democratic leadership hired a "professionally respected staff"; (c) the Democratic leadership "grappled with most of the major issues": (d) the Democratic leadership prevented "further incursions on the Constitution by pressure groups other than the Church"; and (e) the Democratic leadership "finished their deliberations on time" to have the required referendum take place on Election Day 1967.

Putting to one side any question about what Dullea meant when he wrote of "incursions on the Constitution by pressure groups other than the Church" (the presence of which groups some might view as an indispensable part of the democratic process), the Dullea balance sheet hardly indicates that the Convention was "characterized by greatness of achievement."

E. *Another Perspective*

While not mentioned by Dullea in the final section ("Success or Failure") of his Charter Revision book, the following facts that he presents elsewhere in his book under the heading "The Amendment Process" provide another perspective in which to consider the 1967 Convention:

> "When asked in 1977 whether they wanted to convene another Constitutional Convention in 1979, the state's voters defeated the proposal by a margin of over 542,000 votes. ... The image of the 1967 Convention as a wasteful political boondoggle remained fresh in the minds of the voters, and neither public officials nor civic groups wished to be associated with a campaign to resurrect the institution so quickly." (Charter Revision, p. 397)

According to the Oxford Dictionary, the noun "boondoggle" is a term of North American slang that means "a trivial, useless or unnecessary undertaking" or "a dishonest undertaking, a fraud." Dullea does not present any data (other than the defeat of the 1977 referendum by a margin of over 542,000 votes) in support of his statement that the "image of the 1967 Convention as a wasteful political boondoggle remained fresh in the minds of the voters." We prefer to assume that the voters simply were wary in 1977 of a repeat of the 1967 Convention "all-or-nothing" experience.

This much is clear, however: whether the 1967 Convention created an image of a "wasteful political boondoggle" or produced a feeling of wariness about a possible repetition of the 1967 experience, the 1967 Convention certainly did not represent for the people of the State of New York in 1977 any "greatness of achievement." Rather than "*a* magnificent failure" (as Dullea called it in his Book) or "*the* magnificent failure" (as he called it in his 1997 essay in Decision 1997), the 1967 Convention was judged by the voters as a failure the repetition of which is to be avoided in the future.

Indeed, the decision of the voters in 1997 — 30 years after the 1967 Convention's "all or nothing" presentation — against holding a constitutional convention tends to confirm that the New York voters still wish to avoid any repetition of what Dullea ineptly calls "the magnificent failure."

New York, NY
November 1999

April 6, 1999

Dr. Richard P. Nathan, Director
The Nelson A. Rockefeller
Institute of Government
411 State Street
Albany, New York 12203-1003

Re: Commentaries on Henrik N. Dullea, "Charter Revision in the Empire State," Chapter 5, Published by The Rockefeller Institute Press in 1997

Dear Dick:

Chapter 5 of Henrik N. Dullea's book, "Charter Revision in the Empire State," published by The Rockefeller Institute Press in 1997, was recently called to my attention. It discusses the New York Temporary State Commission on the Constitutional Convention (the "Commission") that prepared 15 substantive reports (plus a subject index in a 16th report) for the elected delegates to the 1967 Constitutional Convention in New York.

In purporting to attribute statements and actions to me as Commission Chairman and Louis Lauer as Counsel to the 1966–1967 Commission, Chapter 5 greatly surprised us. Neither Mr. Lauer nor I had ever been interviewed by Mr. Dullea concerning any aspect of the 1966–1967 Commission, its staff, its work product or its or our roles or objectives. Mr. Dullea's failure to seek out such obvious sources of highly relevant information has led him to rely on baseless quotes and attributions and to reach unreliable and misleading conclusions about the work of the 1966–1967 Commission.

As Chairman of the 1966–1967 Commission and Counsel to the 1966–1967 Commission, respectively, I and Mr.

Lauer know that Chapter 5 is erroneous and misleading in important respects. Chapter 5's serious errors and misleading statements are discussed in a Preface and Combined Summary attached to this letter. Those serious and misleading statements are more fully discussed in the two Commentaries, one by Louis Lauer and the other by me, that follow the Preface and Combined Summary.

As you noted in your Foreword to Mr. Dullea's book, the book purports to be not only a scholarly history of events in 1966 and 1967, but instructive to future scholars and the public in considering future such Constitutional Conventions. Cumulatively, however, the serious errors and misleading statements described in the Combined Summary and the two Commentaries demonstrate that Chapter 5 is not based on appropriate scholarly research standards and does not adequately address basic issues of importance in planning for future constitutional conventions in New York State. It is, therefore, essential to set the record straight.

The Rockefeller Institute, a public institution supporting scholarship and education, has a responsibility to insure that its publications provide its readers with accurate and carefully researched essential facts and perspective. Otherwise, future scholars and students of New York constitutional history will not have reliable lessons of the past. It is for these reasons that I strongly urge The Rockefeller Institute to publish Mr. Lauer's and my Commentaries and see that they are also distributed to prior and future recipients of Mr. Dullea's book.

You may wish to send a copy of this letter, the Preface, Combined Summary and two Commentaries to Mr. Dullea. If so, I am forwarding an extra set to you for that purpose.

I look forward to your prompt and favorable response to this request to set the record straight.

Sincerely yours,

Sol Neil Corbin

June 2, 1999

Dr. Richard P. Nathan, Director
The Nelson A. Rockefeller
Institute of Government
411 State Street
Albany, New York 12203-1003

Re: Commentaries on Henrik N. Dullea, "Charter Revision in the Empire State," Chapter 5, Published by The Rockefeller Institute Press in 1997

Dear Dick:

I empathize with your understandable mistake in having relied on, and endorsed as to scholarship in your Foreword, Mr. Dullea's seeming credentials and his representations in his Chapter 5. By Mr. Lauer's and my Commentaries, Mr. Dullea's representations have been proven to be wholly inadequate and substantially erroneous.

On April 6, 1999, I wrote to you with the sincere hope that, in the interests of historical accuracy and scholarship, you would redeem that mistake and reestablish the Institute's purposes by printing and distributing Mr. Lauer's and my Commentaries to the recipients of Mr. Dullea's book. Notwithstanding Mr. Cooper's protestations in his May 12 letter, I continue to urge you to do so.

Contrary to Mr. Cooper's and Mr. Dullea's views in their recent letters (May 12 and May 2, respectively), our Commentaries are not confined to matters of opinion or conclusions about which one can debate. Our Commentaries are largely directed to facts about which there can be no dispute or debate. Those facts overwhelmingly belie Mr. Dullea's speculations and unfounded conclusions in Chapter 5.

No institution is greater than its tools for learning. Accordingly, once again Mr. Lauer and I ask that, in the interests of true scholarship and historical accuracy, you undertake for the Institute to print and distribute our Commentaries.

If, for any reason, you reject that request, this is to inform you that Mr. Lauer and I intend to arrange through other sources for the printing and distribution of our Commentaries in the interests of promoting scholarship and informed discussion of state governmental matters. We would ask that you do the following:

1. Obtain for us Mr. Cooper's and Mr. Dullea's authorization to publish as part of our Commentaries their May letters responding to our Commentaries, and

2. Arrange to provide for us the names and addresses of all persons and institutions who acquired Mr. Dullea's book published by the Institute Press, so that our Commentaries may be distributed to such persons and institutions for their reference and that of their users.

In the latter regard, you may be assured that the lists of names and addresses will be used solely in inviting the acquisition of our Commentaries and for no other purpose.

We would appreciate your prompt response to this letter.

With best regards,

Sincerely,

Sol Neil Corbin

cc: Louis Lauer, Esq.

June 17, 1999

Mr. Sol N. Corbin
Corbin, Silverman and Sanseverino
805 Third Avenue
New York, New York 10022

Dear Sol:

I am writing to respond to your letter of June 2, 1999. It is our position — and this is customary for publishers — that it is not our appropriate role to print and disseminate commentaries on books and other publications we issue. I know this will not please you. But as a person who has devoted my adult life to scholarship on government issues, I am used to the slings and arrows of people who see the world differently from me. You are of course free to publish your commentary, and I think you should do so. As for Hank Dullea's letter to me, you should communicate directly with him as to whether he would give you permission to publish his letter. It is also not our policy to provide information about the purchasers of books.

As a major contributor to substantive policy on the New York State Constitution and also to Nelson A. Rockefeller's record of public service to New York State, I respect you in a special way and deeply regret that this matter causes you such great concern. I am very sorry this difference has arisen and does not seem resolvable in a mutually satisfactory way.

I want you to know that I read your paper carefully, consulted with others about it, including other publishers and legal counsel for the SUNY Research Foundation, and I believe this is the proper response to give to you.

I have no objection to your distributing copies of this letter.

Sincerely,

Richard P. Nathan

Director

Part I
Summary

The two Commentaries that follow this Summary detail the factual errors and misleading statements concerning the Commission contained in Chapter 5 of the Dullea Book. The basic flaw in Chapter 5 is that it proceeds on Dullea's assertion that the Commission was "plagued by partisan divisions" — an assertion this Summary demonstrates is completely false. The two Commentaries also show that many of the factual errors and misleading statements contained in Chapter 5 reflect political spin produced by partisan loyalties, rather than research and analysis produced by disciplined scholarship.

These failings in what purports to be a scholarly work are evident in the Dullea Book's treatment of five areas (in addition to his mistaken characterization of the 1967 Convention as "a magnificient failure"):

1. The Commission's unanimous decision to submit objective reports, without substantive policy recommendations, to the elected Convention delegates;

2. The three-month deadlock over the choice of the Commission's first Executive Director, Ralph Straetz;

3. The resignation of the Commission's first Executive Director two-and-a-half months after his appointment;

4. The quality and usefulness of the Commission's 15 substantive reports, and

5. Corbin's objectives and actions as the Commission's second Chairman (during whose tenure all of the Commission's hearings were held and all of its reports prepared).

1. The Commission's Decision to Present Objective Reports Without Substantive Policy Recommendation

Mr. Dullea states (at p. 133) that:

> "Straetz, reflecting the orientation of the Democratic members (Fisher, Bergan, and Marshall) pressed hard for the endorsement of specific policy recommendations. Corbin, Moore and the other Republicans generally opposed this strategy, arguing instead that the 1966–1967 Commission should limit its efforts to a review of alternatives — a posture somewhat at variance with their earlier stand on the Peck Commission."

This statement is both erroneous and misleading in several respects.

First, as is obvious by the public record, no Republican who was a member of the 1966–1967 Commission had served as a member of the Peck Commission. Therefore, none could have taken any posture at variance with an earlier stand he took on the Peck Commission.

Second, to Mr. Corbin's and Mr. Lauer's knowledge, Mr. Straetz never "pressed," "hard" or otherwise, for the 1966–1967 Commission to endorse specific policy recommendations on substantive issues for consideration by the Convention delegates.

Third, the 1966–1967 Commission members, Democrat and Republican, voted unanimously in support of all of the 1966–1967 Commission's reports that (a) identified the substantive issues for the Convention delegates, (b) discussed objectively and fairly the alternatives in meeting the issues, and (c) set forth reasons both in favor and against each alternative. This approach served to satisfy the 1966–1967 Commission's purpose in facilitating the exercise of the independent judgment of the elected Convention delegates.

Fourth, there never was a stand taken by Commission members over the scope of the 1966–1967 Commission's reports before Mr. Straetz resigned on September 19, 1966. That stand was taken when the 1966–1967 Commission unanimously approved its first report, "1967 Convention Issues," on December 22, 1966, and that stand continued through each of its subsequent reports.

Mr. Dullea also makes the bald statement (at p. 135) that after the appointment of Robert S. Herman as successor to Mr. Straetz, the "Democrats acquiesced to the Republican preference for a listing of alternatives" in the 1966–1967 Commission's reports, and not to make substantive policy recommendations. There is no factual support for this statement.

Moreover, Mr. Dullea's statement at p. 135 is incongruous with his statement at p. 133. If, as Mr. Dullea says, a few Democrats "pressed" for specific policy recommendations before Mr. Straetz resigned, then Mr. Dullea needs to explain why those few Democrats should abandon that position after Mr. Straetz resigned, unless through Mr. Straetz they sought, at the 1966–1967 Commission level, to control the content of the policy recommendations.

The facts are that early in Commission discussions, the 1966–1967 Commission members expressed some sentiment on each side of the question of substantive policy recommendations and Mr. Corbin stated so publicly. However, no stand was taken on the question until later in the 1966–1967 Commission's work and there was never a partisan alignment of "Republicans" and "Democrats" among Commission members on the question.

2. Three-month Deadlock Over Choice of First Executive Director

Mr. Dullea states (at p. 132 of his Book) that first Commission Chairman "Heald went ahead and announced the staff appointments" but "unfortunately, Heald had apparently failed to review his plans in detail with the legislative leaders, and no action was forthcoming on the appropriation" of funds for the 1966–1967 Commission. In doing so, Mr. Dullea does not make plain what really happened.

First, there is no question that Mr. Dullea's opaque term, "legislative leaders," could only have meant one leader — Anthony J. Travia, Speaker of the Assembly. Mr. Dullea should have known that fact because at the time he worked for the Assembly. It was Speaker Travia who refused to appropriate funds for the 1966–1967 Commission because he sought to pressure Chairman Heald to appoint Ralph 1. Straetz as the 1966–1967 Commission's Executive Director.

Second, in fact, Chairman Heald resisted that pressure because he was determined to have a nonpartisan senior staff, whose loyalty did not run to any political figure.

Third, unknown to Mr. Corbin until recently when Mr. Lauer so informed him, Chairman Heald, former Chancellor of New York University, had checked with his sources about Mr. Straetz, who was then employed at New York University, and had concluded that Mr. Straetz was not sufficiently qualified to be the 1966–1967 Commission's Executive Director.

3. Resignation of First Executive Director

Mr. Dullea states (at p. 134) that:

> "Policy conflicts, exacerbated by personality clashes between Straetz and Louis Lauer, led to Straetz's resignation on September 19 amid public recriminations with Corbin. These setbacks were highly demoralizing to the staff...."

Here, again, Mr. Dullea's account is erroneous and misleading in several respects.

First, Mr. Dullea does not specify either any "policy conflicts" or any "personality clashes" with Mr. Lauer. Based on the common understanding of those words, there were no such conflicts or clashes.

Second, Mr. Straetz resigned after he had failed — for a period of over two months and despite Mr. Corbin's repeated requests — to produce a proposed line-item Commission budget for staff and expenses and a proposed research plan so necessary for the 1966–1967 Commission to accomplish its task in the nine months remaining before the Convention commenced in April 1967. As Mr. Corbin stated publicly at the time Mr. Straetz resigned, Mr. Straetz would have been fired for "persisting in a course of disruptive action" if he had not resigned.

Third, Mr. Straetz never complained to Mr. Corbin, nor did he complain to Mr. Lauer, about any such "policy conflicts" or "personality clashes". Mr. Straetz did not give those reasons when he resigned. Indeed, he did not give any reason for resigning in his official letter of resignation. In addition, he never communicated to Mr. Corbin or Mr. Lauer any threat to resign before he submitted his resignation.

Fourth, as to "public recriminations," there was none. In his account, Mr. Dullea, without saying so, conceivably may have been alluding to political campaign comments of certain Democratic candidates then actively seeking the office of Governor or Lieutenant Governor. But those transparently partisan campaign comments do not rise to a level for a disinterested scholar to characterize — without at least disclosing the factual basis for the characterization — as "public recriminations."

Fifth, as to the effect on the 1966–1967 Commission's staff of Mr. Straetz's resignation, as Mr. Lauer states, different members of the staff reacted differently. Rather than being "highly demoralized," members of the Counsel's staff were hopeful that a new Executive Director would be more effective a contributor than Mr. Straetz had been. Members of Mr. Straetz's staff — none of whom resigned concurrently or after Mr. Straetz resigned and none of whom was fired by Mr. Corbin or by Mr. Herman, the new Executive

Director — manifested a "wait-and-see" attitude, but did not seem to be "highly" or otherwise "demoralized".

Sixth, despite the fact that, for three months, Speaker Travia had held up the appropriations to the 1966–1967 Commission over Mr. Heald's refusal to accede to the appointment of Mr. Straetz, the 1966–1967 Commission staff then in office continued to work dedicatedly, although they did not receive any compensation throughout that period. If that inordinate delay in compensation didn't "demoralize" the staff, certainly Mr. Dullea's discussion of the impact on staff of Mr. Straetz's resignation is exaggerated.

4. Quality and Usefulness of Commission Reports

Mr. Dullea reports (in footnote 8 at p. 134) that "interviews with several members of the Convention's leadership lead me to conclude that the 1966–1967 Commission's work and its staff were rapidly forgotten." Yet, as Mr. Lauer notes in his Commentary, in Mr. Dullea's own discussion of the Convention's development of a proposed Bill of Rights later in his book, he contradicts and casts doubt on his breezy statement that the "Commission's work" was "rapidly forgotten." There Mr. Dullea refers at length to one of the "more comprehensive" Commission reports.

Moreover, after the 1966–1967 Commission adopted and published on January 11, 1967 its second report (entitled "Toward an Effective Convention") a sharp controversy arose in the Legislature over whether the Legislature or the Convention itself should adopt the rules regulating lobbyists at the Convention. On this issue, the unanimous views of the 1966–1967 Commission prevailed over those of Speaker Travia, who advocated that the Legislature, rather than the Convention delegates, should prescribe the lobbying rules.

As for Mr. Dullea's statement that the 1966–1967 Commission's "staff" was "rapidly forgotten", Mr. Dullea's omission of any explicit identification — by name, political party affiliation or position — of any of the "several" Convention "leaders" he interviewed prevents an independent assessment of the objectivity and correctness of the interviewees on whom he claims he relied.

Mr. Dullea also states (at p. 134) that his interviews with unidentified persons support a finding that the 1966–1967 Commission's substantive reports were "non-controversial and uneven in quality" and "were not widely used" in "all subject areas".

This sweeping statement is not only contradicted by Mr. Dullea's own later assessment on the proposed Bill of Rights described above, but fails to be based on scholarly research. As Mr. Lauer notes in his Commentary, Dullea's Book does not inquire into or describe any of the subcommittees formed by the 1966–1967 Commission to prepare Commission reports; the superb qualifications of the members of those subcommittees to produce comprehensive, impartial reports; the highly competent consultants retained to assist in the process; Commission policy in the recruitment of staff; the range of subjects covered by the 1966–1967 Commission's reports, and the magnitude of the work product (some 2,000 pages).

In addition, as Mr. Lauer also notes in his Commentary, rather than simply state that the 1966–1967 Commission's thirteen reports on substantive issues before the convention were "uneven in quality", Mr. Dullea's work, if it had complied with scholarly standards, would have gone further. It would have specified what reports, in his judgment or in the judgment of identified interviewees were of "high" quality, what reports were of "medium" quality and what reports, if any, were of "low" quality. The missing descriptive and evaluative information renders Mr. Dullea's sweeping statement concerning 13 Commission reports less than reliable or fair comment.

Lastly, throughout Mr. Dullea's Chapter 5 there runs a current of belief that the 1966–1967 Commission operated in a partisan way — that is, all or a majority of Democrats on one side and all or a majority of Republicans on the other. As Mr. Lauer observes in his Commentary, that was not the case and reflects inadequate scholarly research methods on Mr. Dullea's part.

5. Corbin's Objectives and Actions as Chairman

Mr. Dullea states (at p. 133) that when Mr. Corbin succeeded Mr. Heald as Chairman of the 1966–1967 Commission, "Corbin was sorely distressed to learn that the executive director of 'his' Commission would be Ralph Straetz", who was an active Democrat. There is no factual basis for that erroneous remark.

First, as Mr. Corbin states, he was not "distressed" to learn of Mr. Straetz's appointment because at the time that he informed the Governor that he would serve as Commission Chairman, he had been told that Speaker Travia wanted Mr. Straetz to be appointed Executive Director.

Second, as Mr. Corbin reports, Mr. Straetz's politics did not "distress" him, "sorely" or otherwise. Louis Lauer, appointed as Commission Counsel by Mr. Heald and who continued to serve in that capacity during Mr. Corbin's tenure, was an active Democrat and that never affected Mr.

Corbin's working relationship with Mr. Lauer. Mr. Corbin's only concern was that all Commission staff members be non-partisan and conduct objective research in their work, something Mr. Lauer had made clear to the Counsel's staff.

Most outrageously, Mr. Dullea (at p. 134) also states that:

> The outcome of the election had eliminated Corbin's chance to become Counsel to the President of the Convention, thus wiping out any real interest on his part in using the 1966–1967 Commission to shape an agenda for the Convention and to educate the public on the possibilities for constitutional revision.

This statement is pure fantasy on Mr. Dullea's part and aptly demonstrates Mr. Corbin's and Mr. Lauer's criticisms of the flawed research and political bias reflected in Chapter 5 of his book.

First, as Mr. Corbin states, he never harbored or manifested any interest, intention or aspiration of becoming, seeking or even secretly wishing to be Counsel to the 1967 Convention's President, whether the Convention's President was a Democrat, Republican, Liberal, Conservative or Independent.

Second, as Mr. Corbin states, he never had or manifested any interest, real or otherwise, in using (nor did he use) the 1966–1967 Commission to shape any agenda for the Convention or for any other personal purpose.

Third, as Mr. Lauer reports, there never was the slightest indication in Mr. Corbin's conduct of any interest on his part in becoming Counsel to the Convention President or in using the 1966–1967 Commission to shape an agenda for the 1967 Convention. Indeed, as Mr. Lauer reports, Mr. Corbin's consistent objective — before and after the November 1966 election — was to have the 1966–1967 Commission help educate the public on issues that might arise at the Convention and furnish the elected delegates with materials that would help them make informed judgments in resolving those issues.

In addition, Mr. Dullea states (at p. 134) that:

> Once the Democrats had won control of the convention, the legislative leadership essentially ceased giving serious attention to the Corbin Commission, and its Chairman responded in kind.

Nothing in his Chapter 5 provides any facts or cites any source in support of those assertions. Mr. Dullea does not identify the persons to whom he refers in using the generic term "legislative leadership". Obviously, given Mr. Dullea's relationship with Speaker Travia, that reference must be to Speaker Travia, not Senate Majority Leader Brydges, a Republican. Neither Speaker Travia nor Senate Majority Leader Brydges nor any other legislative leader (minority or majority or key legislative Committee Chairman) ever told Mr. Corbin or Mr. Lauer, nor was any of them quoted as saying, that he ceased giving serious attention to the 1966–1967 Commission.

Second, it is inconceivable that the legislative leaders as a group, having appointed twelve of the eighteen distinguished Commission members (many of whom were also elected as ranking Convention delegates) who prepared the 1966–1967 Commission's substantive reports, would have abandoned the 1966–1967 Commission's efforts.

Third, as Mr. Corbin states, he *never* "responded", in kind or otherwise, to the public views of any legislative leader, except on the merits of the 1966–1967 Commission's Second Report (dealing with the 1966–1967 Commission's legislative and other recommendations for an effective Convention) and Fifth Report (concerning Convention rules for the structure and operations of the Convention). Because of their subject matter, those two reports uniquely required Commission recommendations, and those recommendations were unanimously approved by all members of the 1966–1967 Commission after the Democrats had won control of the 1967 Convention.

Lastly, Mr. Dullea states (at p. 131) that the Governor's appointees to the 1966–1967 Commission, in contrast to the "Democratic appointees," "could be relied on to protect his interests." Mr. Dullea did not bother to specify the Governor's "interests," but in any event, there is no factual basis for this remark. As Mr. Corbin reports, the Governor never discussed his "interests" with him, nor did the Governor ever suggest to him any "interests" that the Governor needed to have protected.

Looking back on Dullea's treament of the five areas discussed in this Summary, it might be too much to say that any single error or single misleading statement, viewed in isolation, evidences political spin produced by partisan loyalties. In our view, when all of those errors and all of those misleading statements are viewed together — in the strange light cast by Dullea's failure to interview the Commission Chairman and the Commission Counsel — it is obvious that the errors and misleading statements reflect political spin produced by partisan loyalties, rather than research and analysis produced by disciplined scholarship.

Part II
CORBIN'S COMMENTARY

1. Introduction

As a member and as Chairman of the 1966–1967 Commission, I know that Chapter 5 of Dullea's book, Charter Revision, is erroneous and misleading in important respects. As the Dullea Book purports to be not only a scholarly history of events in 1966 and 1967, but instructive to future scholars and the public in considering future Constitutional Conventions,[3] it is essential to set the record straight.

In Chapter 5, Mr. Dullea purports to attribute statements and actions to me and Louis Lauer (who had served as Counsel to the 1966–1967 Commission throughout its existence). Yet neither of us was ever interviewed by Mr. Dullea concerning any aspect of the Commission, its staff, its work product, its role or its or our roles or objectives.

Mr. Lauer and I strongly believe that Mr. Dullea's failure to seek relevant information from us has led him to produce a flawed discussion and to reach unreliable and misleading conclusions about our respective roles and the work of the

---

3 See the Foreword to the Dullea Book written by Richard P. Nathan, Director of The Nelson A. Rockefeller Institute of Government.

1966–1967 Commission. Mr. Dullea's account in Chapter 5 provides neither essential facts nor perspective to readers that will allow them to reach conclusions other than those Mr. Dullea has adopted. Accordingly, Mr. Lauer and I were prompted to write separate commentaries, based on personal knowledge and public documents, to correct the record. Mr. Lauer's Commentary follows this Commentary.

Mr. Lauer and I have not written to vindicate our roles or the work of the 1966–1967 Commission. The 15 reports of the Commission, comprising about 2,000 pages of analytical research useful to any student of the New York State constitutional record, speak for themselves.

We write because future scholars and students of the subject deserve accurate and carefully researched lessons of the past. Future agencies and proponents of constitutional change should be able to rely upon a fairly-presented written history. Mr. Lauer and I know from personal experience that Mr. Dullea's Chapter 5 badly fails to meet that requirement of reliability.

2. Correcting and Supplementing Dullea's Flawed Discussion of the Commission

A. *The Circumstances Leading to my Becoming a Member in 1965 and Chairman of the 1966–1967 Commission*

In September 1965, after having served as Counsel to Governor Nelson A. Rockefeller for over three years, I resigned in order to return to the private practice of law. In November 1965, the voters of New York State approved a referendum calling for a convention to revise the State's Constitution. In December of that year, the Governor asked me to become one of his six appointees to the newly-created Commission. He proposed as Commission Chairman, Mr. Harold T. Heald, a most distinguished citizen and public servant who had been Chancellor of New York University and President of the Ford Foundation. I agreed to serve and was designated as one of eighteen members of the 1966–1967 Commission.

Based upon facts known to me, Mr. Lauer, in his accompanying Commentary, has accurately and completely described Mr. Heald's tenure and the circumstances leading to his resignation as Chairman.

B. *Chairman Heald's Reasons for Not Appointing Mr. Straetz*

Mr. Dullea states (at p. 132 of his book) that Commission Chairman "Heald went ahead and announced the staff appointments" but "unfortunately, Heald had apparently failed to review his plans in detail with the legislative leaders, and no action was forthcoming on the appropriation" of funds for the 1966–1967 Commission. In doing so, Mr. Dullea obfuscates what really happened and had he interviewed Mr. Lauer and me, he would have gotten his facts straight.

Following Mr. Heald's resignation at the end of June 1966, the Governor consulted with Anthony J. Travia, the Speaker of the Assembly, a Democrat who knew me well after I had worked closely with him in carrying out the Governor's legislative program when I had been Counsel to the Governor. I was later informed that he consented to the Governor's proposal that I become Chairman of the Commission.

During the first week of July 1996, the Governor asked me to succeed Mr. Heald and serve as Chairman. I then was told by the Governor that Speaker Travia wanted Mr. Ralph A. Straetz to become Executive Director of the Commission. I agreed to serve, if elected, as Chairman, but I was not aware that, as disclosed in Mr. Lauer's Commentary, Mr. Heald had earlier refused to appoint Mr. Straetz because of the negative report he had received about Mr. Straetz's qualifications. I did know then, however, that from April to July of 1966 Speaker Travia had held up the reappropriation of funds for the 1966–1967 Commission's operations because of Mr. Heald's refusal to appoint Mr. Straetz.

Thus, there is no question that Mr. Dullea's reference to "legislative leaders" could only have meant Speaker Travia, who sought to pressure Chairman Heald to appoint Mr. Straetz as the Commission's Executive Director. There were two reasons for Mr. Heald's refusal to accede to Speaker Travia's pressure. First, Chairman Heald resisted that pressure because he was determined to have a senior staff function in a nonpartisan manner, one whose loyalty did not run to any political figure, . Second, as Mr. Lauer recently so informed me, Chairman Heald, former Chancellor of New York University, had checked with his sources about Mr. Straetz, who was then employed at New York University, and had concluded that Mr. Straetz was not sufficiently qualified to be the Commission's Executive Director.

C. *Mr. Straetz's Appointment*

Mr. Dullea states (at p. 133) that when I succeeded Mr. Heald as Chairman of the 1966–1967 Commission, "Corbin was sorely distressed to learn that the executive director of 'his' Commission would be Ralph Straetz", who was an active Democrat. There is no factual basis for that erroneous remark.

I was not "distressed" to learn of Mr. Straetz's appointment because, as noted above, at the time that I informed the Governor I would serve as Commission Chairman, I had been told that Speaker Travia wanted Mr. Straetz to be appointed Executive Director. I would never have taken on the burden of Chairman if, at the outset, I had been "distressed" about having Mr. Straetz serve in such an important position.

Also, as Counsel to the Governor I was accustomed to working constructively with active Democrats, and Mr. Straetz's politics did not "distress" me, "sorely" or otherwise.

In addition, I was not aware that Mr. Straetz was a member of any Democratic Advisory Committee, but, if so, that would not have "distressed" me, "sorely" or otherwise. Mr. Lauer, appointed as Commission Counsel by Mr. Heald and who continued to serve during my tenure as Chairman, was an active Democrat and that never affected my working relationship with him; I could rely on his professionalism. My only concern was that all Commission staff members be non-partisan in their work, something Mr. Lauer had made clear to the Counsel's staff.

Finally, I never used the possessive case in referring to the 1966–1967 Commission. Although the media and, indeed, Mr. Dullea (at p. 134) referred to the Commission as the "Corbin Commission" as short-hand for the Commission's longer, more formal name, I never referred to it as the "Corbin Commission" or "my" Commission.

D. *My Experience with Mr. Straetz*

Before and promptly after I became Chairman of the Commission on July 11, 1966, I spoke with Mr. Lauer. He briefed me on his progress in researching the history of prior Constitutional Conventions, the existing provisions and judicial interpretations of the Constitution and the likely issues involved in proposed changes. We both were in awe of the amount and breadth of work necessary for the 1966–1967 Commission to make a comprehensive study and reports for the elected Convention delegates who were scheduled to assemble on April 4, 1967, a bare nine months later.

I then met with Mr. Lauer and Mr. Straetz, who, on July 11, 1966, succeeded Richard Atkins, Mr. Heald's appointee, as staff director. As an organizational matter, I asked Mr. Straetz to prepare a proposed line-item budget for staff and expenses within the combined $800,000 lump-sum appropriations ($150,000 in reappropriations of 1965 appropriations and $650,000 of 1966 appropriations) for the 1966–1967 Commission's work. Most important, I also asked Mr. Straetz to prepare a proposed research plan for the Commission to accomplish its assigned task. I asked that his combined proposed budget and research plan be discussed with Mr. Lauer and be available for my review in early August, following my return from a pre-arranged vacation.

About the second week of August, after my return from vacation, I met with Messrs. Straetz and Lauer in order to receive a report on Mr. Straetz's proposed budget and research plan for the Commission's consideration. Mr. Straetz produced no plan, but indicated that he needed more time to do so, which I gave him, knowing of the importance of the plan to me, the Commission members and its staff.

Another month passed and I still had not received Mr. Straetz's proposed budget and research plan. Finally, highly concerned, I asked him to produce one by Saturday September 17, when I scheduled a meeting with him and Mr. Lauer.

E. *Mr. Straetz's Resignation*

Mr. Straetz did not deliver a plan or even appear for the meeting on Saturday morning, September 17. Earlier that morning, I had heard from a friendly source that Mr. Straetz was resigning as Executive Director.

The following Monday, September 19, I went early to the Commission's offices and asked Mr. Straetz's secretary whether Mr. Straetz "had left anything for me." In response, his secretary handed over to me a photocopy of an unsigned, long and angry letter of resignation that had been prepared by Mr. Straetz.

Later on Monday morning, September 19, upon receipt of an inquiry from a reporter of *The New York Times* concerning Mr. Straetz's resignation and his reasons for resigning, I released the text of Mr. Straetz's letter given to me by his secretary. The letter, which I read to the *Times* reporter at the time but regrettably did not later retain, purported to recite Mr. Straetz's stated grievances:

(1) I had in general "created confusion" and had tried to tell him "how to conduct research," making his work "both demeaning and intolerable."

(2) The position of Executive Director "has been made one which no reputable scholar-administrator would retain since he would not accept responsibility for an operation over which he had no control."

(3) My "demand" that he "share equal authority" with Mr. Lauer had "created a two-headed monster with almost continuous conflict on almost every" issue.[4]

As also reported in the Times news article, the following was my response to these grievances:

(1) Mr. Straetz "quit for the record" because "he would have been fired for persisting in a course of disruptive action" — an allusion to his failure and refusal to produce the requested proposed budget and research plan.

(2) He was seeking "to inject politics into a non-partisan Commission" and to "arrogate total authority to himself."

(3) Mr. Straetz was not hired to "control" the 1966–1967 Commission in doing its work of preparing reports for the Convention delegates. "He was to be a staff person helping the Commission" to do its work.

4 *The New York Times*, September 20, 1966, p. 1, col. 8.

(4) Concerning his refusal to share authority with Mr. Lauer, the Commission's Counsel, my view was that the input of a "lawyer was needed to give legal interpretation" of the Constitution's provisions and the "political scientist's job" was "to see if the Constitution satisfies desired objectives."[5]

Subsequent to my conversation, the Times reporter called me back to advise me that Mr. Straetz later that day stated to the reporter that his "official" letter of resignation merely said "I hereby resign as executive director of the Temporary State Commission on the Constitutional Convention, as of today".[6] Mr. Straetz also had told the reporter that his resignation letter was put in the mail late on September 19, 1966,[7] the very day I had answered the reporter's original inquiry.

Fortunately, the 1966–1967 Commission staff, consisting of a group of lawyers and a separate group of social and political scientists, had continued their work. In addition, one month later, on October 19, Robert S. Herman, with whom I had previously worked for many years, was appointed as Executive Director by the Commission, based upon the unanimous recommendation of a four-member subcommittee of the Commission. Mr. Herman did not "control" the Commission "operation," as advocated by Mr. Straetz. Mr. Herman, accustomed to working with lawyers and more knowledgeable than Mr. Straetz about the Constitution, had no apparent difficulty in working with Mr. Lauer

5 *Id.*

6 *Id.*

7 *Id.*

and his legal staff, nor did Mr. Herman's research staff, as is evidenced by the Commission's 15 substantive reports.

F. *The Question of Specific Policy Recommendations*

Mr. Dullea also states (at p. 133) that:

> "Straetz, reflecting the orientation of the Democratic members (Fisher, Bergan, and Marshall) pressed hard for the endorsement of specific policy recommendations. Corbin, Moore and the other Republicans generally opposed this strategy, arguing instead that the Commission should limit its efforts to a review of alternatives — a posture somewhat at variance with their earlier stand on the Peck Commission."

This statement is both erroneous and misleading in several respects.

First, as is obvious by the public record available to any researcher, no Republican who was a member of the 1966–1967 Commission had served as a member of the Peck Commission. Therefore, none could have taken any posture at variance with an earlier stand he took on the Peck Commission.

Second, Mr. Straetz never, in my presence, "pressed," "hard" or otherwise, for the Commission to endorse specific policy recommendations on substantive issues for consideration by the Convention delegates. Mr. Straetz never produced a research plan, much less defined any issues or identified any possible policy position or recommendations.

Third, Mr. Dullea refers to only three of the nine Democrats then serving as Commission members as supporting specific policy recommendations. By his account the other Democrats (a large majority of the Democrats) evidently were opposed to or silent on making specific policy recommendations to the elected Convention delegates.

Fourth, the 1966–1967 Commission members, Democrat and Republican, voted unanimously in support of all of the Commission's reports which identified the substantive issues for the Convention delegates. These reports discussed fairly and objectively the alternatives in meeting the issues, and set forth reasons both in favor and against each alternative, leaving specific policy decisions on the substantive issues to be freely debated and made by the elected delegates.

Fifth, there never was a stand taken by Commission members over the scope of the 1966–1967 Commission's reports before Mr. Straetz resigned on September 19, 1996. That stand was taken when the Commission unanimously approved its first report, on Convention Issues, published on December 22, 1966, and that stand continued through each of its subsequent reports.

Finally — and without justification — the Dullea Book implicitly suggests that partisan political considerations led the nine Democratic and nine Republican members of the Commission unanimously to decide not to make substantive policy recommendations to the elected 1967 Convention delegates. My clear recollection of discussions with Commission members is to the contrary. Indeed, as the following chronology demonstrates, the Commission simply did not have enough time (1) to make objective comprehensive studies of the detailed New York Constitution *and* (2) to resolve substantive policy issues involving — to name only a few controversial issues in 1966-67 — church-state relations; the requirement of a referendum for incurrence of state debt; the organization of the court system and methods of judicial selection; and state-local governmental relations.

Compelled by developments outside its control and mindful of its only statutory mandate (to prepare a "comprehensive study"), the Commission unanimously voted on December 22, 1965 to prepare impartial briefing papers to assist the elected Convention delegates resolve the substantive issues of policy.

The relevant chronology, beginning with the June 14, 1965 legislation that resulted in a November 1965 referendum in favor of a Constitutional Convention, follows:

1. *Legislation for a preparatory commission.* On June 24, 1965 (ten days after the enactment of legislation calling for a referendum on whether to hold a constitutional convention), a statute was enacted that authorized an 18-member preparatory commission. Scheduled to expire on March 31, 1966, this statute provided for the Commission to prepare a "comprehensive study" on the Constitution, but did not require the Commission to make substantive policy recommendations to the delegates.

2. *Vote for a convention; appointment of commission members.* The Commission was *not* appointed until some time after the voters at the general election in November 1965 approved the proposal to hold a Constitutional Convention. Indeed, it was not until December 19, 1965 that the Governor, the Senate Majority Leader and the Speaker of the Assembly each appointed six Commissioners, all of

whom served without compensation. This timetable presumably was designed to avoid a repetition of New York's 1957 experience, when a preparatory commission was authorized and organized before the referendum on whether to hold a constitutional convention — and the voters decided against holding a convention. In any event, after the enactment of the June 1965 legislation that authorized the Commission, some six months passed without the appointment of Commission members to commence the work that might have made it feasible for the Commission to do a comprehensive objective study *and* make substantive policy recommendations to the elected delegates.

3. *Commission experience from December 19, 1965 to July, 1966.* As reported in the Dullea Book (at p. 131), the Commission held its first organizational meeting on January 20, 1966 — one month after its members were appointed — and elected Mr. Heald, who had been appointed by Governor Rockefeller, as Chairman. It was then clear that the membership of the Commission was likely to change to take into account the 1965 election that shifted control of the State Senate from the Democrats to the Republicans. There was thus some uncertainty whether the six members appointed in December 1965 by Democratic Senator Zaretzki would be reappointed by the new Majority Leader, Republican Senator Brydges.

With little more than 14 months remaining from the January 20, 1966 organizational meeting of the Commission until the mandated April 4, 1967 opening of the Constitutional Convention, Mr. Heald began to assemble staff and appointed a Study Director and Counsel. As is discussed in detail elsewhere in this Commentary and in the Lauer Commentary, he was asked on April 1, 1996 to appoint Speaker

Travia's candidate, Ralph Straetz, as Executive Director. His refusal to do so led Speaker Travia to hold up any appropriation of funds for the Commission.

The Heald-Travia contretemps lasted until Mr. Heald resigned in June 1966. Then, in early July, 1996 — more than a year after the enactment of legislation authorizing the Commission and less than nine months before the elected Convention delegates were to meet — some new members were appointed to the Commission (in place of three appointees of Senator Zaretzki); Speaker Travia's candidate, Ralph Straetz, was appointed as the Commission's Executive Director; I was elected as the Commission's new Chairman, and funds were appropriated to the Commission.

4. *Commission experience from July 1996 to October 1996.* As is also detailed in this Commentary and in Lauer's, Ralph Straetz never prepared a proposed budget and research program for my consideration and submission to the Commission, although I had repeatedly asked him to do so. He formally resigned on September 19, 1966 — some six-and-a-half months before the elected Convention delegates were to convene on April 4, 1967. The Commission was thus required to function without an Executive Director for about another month, until Robert S. Herman (who had served in the State Division of the Budget during the Harriman and Rockefeller Administrations) was appointed the Commission's new Executive Director. At that point, less than six months remained until the elected Convention delegates were to convene on April 4, 1967.

5. *Commission action from October 1966 to December 22, 1996.* The Commission held four public hearings in October 1996. It was after these public hearings that the

Commission — with less than six months remaining before the delegates were to convene — met in Subcommittees and then as a Commission to review the issues involved in a "comprehensive study" of the Constitution. On December 22, 1966 — with little more than three months remaining before the delegates were to meet — the Commission approved its first report, "1967 Convention Issues."

The Commission then proceeded to submit two procedural reports, respectively containing recommendations on legislation needed to enable the Convention to function effectively and on rules for the organization and operation of the Convention. In addition, it prepared thirteen reports — all reviewed and approved by the Commission in the three months starting on December 22, 1966 with its first report — that defined substantive constitutional issues, provided relevant factual material, and discussed alternative solutions and the arguments for and against each alternative. In doing so, the Commission unanimously decided not to make substantive policy recommendations.

In view of this chronology of events and the range of issues to be considered in a "comprehensive" review of the New York Constitution, it is more than fair to say that, as a practical matter, time did not permit the Commission — as knowledgeable as its members were — (1) to prepare objective reports discussing for the benefit of the elected delegates the pros and cons of many complicated constitutional issues, *and* (2) even if it wish to, to take substantive positions on those issues before the elected Convention delegates gathered on April 4, 1967. The second of these two functions was not achievable within the time constraints under which the Commission was compelled to do its job.

G. *Personality "Clashes" and "Public Recriminations"*

Mr. Dullea states (at p. 134) that:

> "Policy conflicts, exacerbated by personality clashes between Straetz and Louis Lauer, led to Straetz's resignation on September 19 amid public recriminations with Corbin. These setbacks were highly demoralizing to the staff...."

Here, again, Mr. Dullea's account is erroneous and misleading in several respects.

First, Mr. Dullea does not specify either any "policy conflicts" or any "personality clashes" between Mr. Straetz and Mr. Lauer. Based on the common understanding of those words, there were no such conflicts or clashes.

Second, Mr. Straetz resigned after he had failed — for a period of over two months and despite my repeated requests — to produce a proposed line-item Commission budget for staff and expenses and a proposed research plan for the Commission to accomplish its task in the nine months remaining before the Convention commenced in April 1967.

Third, Mr. Straetz never complained to me, nor did he complain to Mr. Lauer, about any such "policy conflicts" or "personality clashes". When he resigned, Mr. Straetz did not give those reasons in the photocopy of his unsigned resignation letter his secretary gave to me. Indeed, he did not give any reason for resigning in his *official* letter of resignation. In addition, he never communicated to me (or as Mr. Lauer reports, to him) any threat to resign before he submitted his resignation.

Fourth, as to "public recriminations," there were none, as Mr. Lauer reports. In his account, Mr. Dullea, without saying so, conceivably may have been alluding to political campaign comments of certain Democratic candidates then seeking the office of Governor or Lieutenant Governor. But those transparently partisan campaign comments do not rise to a level for a disinterested scholar to characterize them — without at least disclosing the factual basis for the characterization —as "public recriminations."

Fifth, as to the effect on the 1966–1967 Commission's staff, as Mr. Lauer states in his Commentary, different members of the staff reacted differently. Rather than being "highly demoralized," members of the Counsel's staff — who had been concerned by Mr. Straetz's apparently limited knowledge of New York's constitutional history and of the materials that delegates would need to review the detailed rules and broad policies into which its Constitution had evolved — were hopeful that a new Executive Director would be more effective a contributor than Mr. Straetz had been. Members of Mr. Straetz's staff — none of whom resigned concurrently or after Mr. Straetz resigned and none of whom was fired by me or Mr. Herman — manifested a "wait-and-see" attitude, but also did not seem to be "highly" or otherwise "demoralized".

As to the balance of Mr. Dullea's narrative concerning Mr. Straetz's resignation, I share and adopt Mr. Lauer's recitation of the facts he recites in his Commentary. I would only add two facts:

(1) From the start of my role as Chairman I had publicly expressed the following:

"The Commission had not decided yet" whether to deliver to the Convention delegates "a package of suggested changes in the Constitution or a study of possible changes, with pros and cons" from which the delegates "could choose."

"Right now [July 12, 1966] we feel we'd serve a more useful purpose by not being advocates of specific proposals."[8]

Obviously, as a long-term student of the New York State Constitution, including during the period I served as Counsel to the Governor, I also had my own personal view on the subject of constitutional simplification. I suggested a two-part Constitution, with simplification based on two different methods of amendment, but I made it clear that I was speaking for myself, not the members of the 1966–1967 Commission.[9].

(2) The 1966–1967 Commission, in preparing its reports on constitutional issues, unanimously adopted the view that it served best by approving a series of reports that (a) raised possible constitutional changes, (b) discussed objectively and fairly the reasons both favoring and opposed to those

8 *The New York Times*, July 12, 1966, p. 24, col. 1-5. See also, The New York Times, October 13, 1966, p. 39.

9 *The New York Times*, August 14, 1966. That method of simplification, incidentally, was shared by my eminent mentor and constitutional scholar, Judge Charles D. Breitel (*The New York Times*, January 28, 1967), who was then a member of the States highest Court, the Court of Appeals, and was former Counsel to Governor Thomas E. Dewey. I had served as law clerk to Judge Breitel early in my legal career when he was an Associate Justice of the Appellate Division (First Department). See my biographical information attached as an Appendix at p. 146 of this Book.

changes, and (c) left it to the duly elected Convention delegates to decide which course to take. Specifically, by approving each of those 13 reports on substantive constitutional issues beginning in late December 1966, the Commission unanimously decided not to recommend specific constitutional changes to the Convention delegates.

H. *The "Chance to Become" Counsel to the Convention President*

Most outrageously, Mr. Dullea (at p. 134) states that:

> The outcome of the election had eliminated Corbin's chance to become Counsel to the President of the Convention, thus wiping out any real interest on his part in using the Commission to shape an agenda for the Convention and to educate the public on the possibilities for constitutional revision."

This statement, not reciting facts but purporting to probe my mind, is pure fantasy on Mr. Dullea's part. It is but another example of Mr. Dullea's dubious research methods.

First, so that the record is clear, I never had or manifested any interest, intention or aspiration of becoming, seeking or even secretly wishing to be Counsel to the 1967 Convention's President, whether the Convention's President was a Democrat, Republican, Liberal, Conservative, Independent or nonpartisan.

Second, I never had or manifested any interest, real or otherwise, in using (nor did I use) the 1966–1967 Commission to shape any agenda for the Convention or for any other personal purpose. I did seek, as did the other members of the Commission, to educate the Convention delegates and the public — through four public hearings and 15 reports totalling nearly 2,000 pages — on the possible issues for constitutional revision, as that was the very purpose of the Commission and the subject of all its reports.

I. *Partisan Acquiescence Concerning Substantive Policy Recommendations*

Mr. Dullea makes the bald statement (at p. 135) that after the appointment of Robert S. Herman as successor to Mr. Straetz, the "Democrats acquiesced to the Republican preference for a listing of alternatives" in the 1966–1967 Commission's reports, and not to make substantive policy recommendations. There is no factual support for this statement. Moreover, Mr. Dullea's statement is incongruous with his statement quoted on page 57. If, as he says, the minority of Democrats and Mr. Straetz "pressed" for specific policy recommendations *before* Mr. Straetz resigned, then Mr. Dullea needs to explain why those few Democrats should abandon that position after he resigned unless, through Mr. Straetz, they sought, at the Commission level, to control the content of the policy recommendations.

The question of whether (a) to issue Commission recommendations on constitutional changes or (b) to list alternatives for change and the advantages and disadvantages of each change was never either connected with Mr. Herman's appointment or a subject of a partisan political split among Commission members. The decision not to make policy recommendations was not a matter of "acquiescence" or "preference," but was made unanimously by the Commission members, Democrat and Republican, in approving its 13 substantive reports.

Early in Commission discussions, the 1966–1967 Commission members expressed some sentiment on each side of the question of substantive policy recommendations and as I noted on pp. 64–65, I stated so publicly. However, no stand was taken on the question until the Commission reports were adopted, and there was never a partisan alignment of "Republicans" and "Democrats" among Commission members on the question.

J. *The Impact of the Commission's Work and Its Staff*

Mr. Dullea reports (in a footnote 8 at p. 134) that "interviews with several members of the Convention's leadership lead me to conclude that the Commission's work and its staff were rapidly forgotten." Yet, as Mr. Lauer reports in his Commentary, in Mr. Dullea's own discussion of the Convention's development of a proposed Bill of Rights later in his book (at pp. 253-256), he contradicts and casts doubt on his breezy statement that the "Commission's work" was "rapidly forgotten." There Mr. Dullea refers at length to one of the "more comprehensive" Commission reports.

As for Mr. Dullea's statement that the Commission's "staff" was "rapidly forgotten", Mr. Dullea's omission of any explicit identification — by name, political party affiliation or position — of any of the "several" Convention "leaders" he interviewed prevents an independent assessment of the objectivity and correctness of the interviewees on whom he indicates he relied.

K. *The Quality of the Commission's Reports*

Mr. Dullea states (at p. 134) that his interviews with unidentified persons support a finding that the 1966–1967 Commission's substantive reports were "non-controversial and uneven in quality" and "were not widely used" in "all subject areas". This sweeping statement is not only contradicted by Mr. Dullea's own later assessment described above in item J, but fails to be based on serious research. As Mr. Lauer notes in his Commentary, the Dullea Book does not inquire into or describe any of the subcommittees formed by the Commission to prepare Commission reports; the superb qualifications of the members of those subcommittees to produce comprehensive, impartial reports; the consultants retained to assist in the process; Commission policy in the recruitment of staff; the range of subjects covered by the Commission's reports, and the magnitude of the work (some 2,000 pages).

In addition, as also noted by Mr. Lauer in his Commentary, rather than state that the Commission's thirteen substantive reports were "uneven in quality", Mr. Dullea's work, if it had complied with scholarly standards, would have gone further. It would have specified what reports, in his judgment or in the judgment of identified interviewees (identified by name, political party affiliation or Convention position) were of "high" quality, what reports were of "medium" quality and what reports, if any, were of "low" quality. The missing descriptive and evaluative information renders Mr. Dullea's sweeping statement concerning 13 Commission reports less than reliable or fair comment.

L. *The Reaction of the "Legislative Leadership" to the Commission*

Mr. Dullea states (at p. 134) that:

> "Once the Democrats had won control of the convention, the legislative leadership essentially

ceased giving serious attention to the Corbin Commission, and its Chairman responded in kind."

Nothing in his Chapter 5 provides any facts or cites any source in support of those assertions. Mr. Dullea does not identify the persons to whom he refers in using the generic term "legislative leadership". Obviously, given Mr. Dullea's relationship with Speaker Travia, that reference must be to Speaker Travia, not Senate Majority Leader Brydges, a Republican. Neither Speaker Travia nor Senate Majority Leader Brydges or any other legislative leader ever told me, nor was any of them quoted as saying that he ceased giving serious attention to the 1966–1967 Commission.

Second, it is inconceivable that the legislative leaders as a group, having appointed twelve of the eighteen distinguished Commission members (many of whom were also elected as ranking Convention delegates) who prepared the 1966–1967 Commission's substantive reports, would have abandoned the Commission's efforts.

Third, I *never* "responded", "in kind" or otherwise, to the public views of any legislative leader, except on the merits of the Commission's Second Report (dealing with the Commission's legislative and other recommendations for an effective Convention)[10] and Fifth Report (concerning Convention rules for the structure and operations of the Convention). Because of their subject matter, those two reports uniquely required Commission recommendations, and those recommendations were *unanimously* approved by all members of the 1966–1967 Commission.

10 *The New York Times*, January 17, 1967, p. 17, col. 1, February 1, 1967, p. 45, col. 2, and February 8, 1967, p. 35, col. 2.

M. *The Governor's "Interests"*

Mr. Dullea states (at p. 131) that the Governor's appointees to the 1966–1967 Commission, in contrast to the "Democratic appointees," "could be relied on to protect his interests." Mr. Dullea did not bother to specify the Governor's "interests," or how those interests differed from those of Democrats, but in any event, there is no factual basis for this remark. The Governor never discussed his "interests" with me, nor did the Governor ever suggest to me any "interests" that the Governor needed to have protected.

In summary, the cumulative effect of these criticisms demonstrates that Chapter 5 of the Dullea Book should not be relied upon by scholars or by future agencies or proponents of constitutional change.

Part III
Lauer's Commentary

1. Introduction

Sol Neil Corbin, the second Chairman of the 1966–1967 Commission, early this year told me that The Rockefeller Institute Press published in 1997 Henrik N. Dullea's *Charter Revision in the Empire State: The Politics of New York's 1967 Constitutional Convention*, Chapter 5 of which discusses the 1966-67 Commission. I served as Counsel to the Commission, having been appointed to that position by Henry T. Heald, its first Chairman, and continued in that position by Mr. Corbin.

As Mr. Dullea has never been in contact with me — the one senior member of the 1966–1967 Commission's staff who served from the Commission's earliest days until the completion of its work — I was surprised by Mr. Corbin's news and confessed that I had not heard of the book before then. When I then told Mr. Corbin that Mr. Dullea had never communicated with me in any way concerning the Commission, Mr. Corbin told me that Mr. Dullea also had not in any way discussed the Commission with him.

Having spent some 15 months of my life on the 1966–1967 Commission's activities and many more in academia, I was puzzled that an author of what purported to be a scholarly work would write about the 1966–1967 Commission without contacting the person who was its Chairman for most of its life and without contacting the one senior member of staff who had served under both of its Chairmen. So, I asked Mr. Corbin to send me a copy of Chapter 5 to see what Mr. Dullea had written. He was kind enough to send me a copy of the chapter along with a copy of the foreword, written by Richard P. Nathan, Director, of The Nelson A. Rockefeller Institute of Government.

I regret to have to report that I found Mr. Dullea's discussion of the 1966–1967 Commission misleadingly incomplete and in important respects erroneous. That discussion also seemed at times to be a politically partisan presentation rather than the disinterested analysis I had expected of a study published by The Rockefeller Institute Press. Hence, while I am no longer involved in government service and no longer actively participate in party politics, I concluded that it would be useful for scholars in the future to have a Commentary, based on my personal knowledge, that corrects and supplements Mr. Dullea's discussion of the 1996-97 Commission.

To enable the reader to make an informed judgment concerning my objectivity, I begin with an autobiographical note on how I came to be appointed Counsel; my political affiliation; my academic and professional experience; and my relationship with Mr. Corbin. This Commentary then corrects and supplements in chronological order the history of the 1966-67 Commission so misleadingly presented in Mr. Dullea's book.

2. Lauer's Biographical Data

A. *My Appointment as Counsel to the 1966–1967 Commission*

My appointment as Counsel to the 1966-1967 Commission, effective April 1, 1966, came about in the following way:

Walter Gellhorn, Professor of Law at Columbia Law School, told me around February 1966 that he had recommended my appointment to a senior staff position with the Commission. A 1953 graduate of Columbia Law School (awarded the Prize in Administrative Law on Professor Gellhorn's recommendation), I was then serving as Director of the Columbia University Project for Effective Justice. That Project pioneered the use of quantitative methods in studying various aspects of the administration of justice.

In the intervening years, I had (in addition to private law practice) taught at Columbia Law School; served as assistant counsel to the Temporary State Commission on the Courts, which proposed a constitutional amendment to reorganize the New York court system; served as an enlisted man in the U.S. Army; been Law Clerk to Judge Harold R. Medina on the U.S. Court of Appeals; collaborated with Professor Gellhorn on pioneering studies of congressional and administrative settlement of tort claims against the United States; co-authored with Professor Gellhorn a study of workmen's compensation in New York State, which led Governor Nelson A. Rockefeller to appoint a committee to review our recommendations; and served as assistant counsel to the Joint Legislative Committee on Court Reorganization, which drafted legislation implementing the constitutional amendment proposed by the Temporary

Commission on the Courts. At the time of my conversation with Professor Gellhorn, I was also serving as Consultant on the Family Court for the New York State Judicial Conference and as Counsel to the Family Court Judges Rules Committee established under the Family Court Act.

Because Professor Gellhorn had been Chairman of the 1958 Inter-Law School Committee on Constitutional Simplification, I assumed that his recommendation would be given serious consideration. That assumption was confirmed when I was called shortly afterwards by Henry T. Heald, first Chairman of the 1966-67 Commission. Mr. Heald told me that I was under consideration for appointment as Counsel to the Commission and invited me to have lunch with him to discuss that possible appointment.

At lunch, Mr. Heald (formerly Chancellor of New York University, later head of the Ford Foundation and at the time of our lunch a prominent educational consultant) told me that he was determined to run a nonpartisan commission that would submit impartial reports to those elected by the voters to be delegates to the Constitutional Convention. He continued that he had been led to believe by those who had recommended me for the position and from what he had heard of my work with the Temporary State Commission on the Courts, the Joint Legislative Committee on Court Reorganization and the Judicial Conference that I would be able to function in that way.

Knowing that Mr. Heald had been appointed by a Republican Governor and determined to avoid any misunderstanding, I immediately told him that I had been active in the reform movement in the Democratic Party and was a registered Democrat (which I still am). At the same time, I told him that I felt comfortable functioning in a disciplined professional manner and completely agreed with his determination to run a nonpartisan commission. He and I then agreed that each of us would further consider my possible appointment as Counsel.

Mr. Heald never told me what further steps, if any, he took in deciding to offer me the position. I discussed the possible appointment with my wife, Professor Gellhorn and close friends.

I also discussed my possible appointment with William vanden Heuvel, then a member of the 1966–1967 Commission, who called me with knowledge that I was about to be asked to become Counsel. (We had known one another when we were both active in the New York Young Democrats, and I had read that he had been appointed to the 1966–1967 Commission on recommendation of Senator Robert F. Kennedy.) Mr. vanden Heuvel said that he thought that the work of the Commission was of such importance that I should undertake the assignment even if I would have to resign from my position at Columbia Law School (as I indeed did have to do) to accept the appointment.

Soon after my lunch meeting with Mr. Heald, he called to offer me the position and invited me to the meeting of the Commission scheduled to be held on April 1, 1966. I accepted and promptly met with William C. Warren, then Dean of Columbia Law School, to resign as Director of the Project for Effective Justice and arrange a smooth transition for my successor. (I later joked, when I worked for the Commission without receiving pay from April 1 to mid-July 1996, that the April 1, 1966 meeting, at which I first learned that the Commission's appropriation had expired the day before, was held on April Fool's Day. As I discuss later in this Commentary, the Commission's appropriation was held up until mid-July 1996.)

B. *Government Experience*

Because a major issue presented in Chapter 5 of Dullea's Charter Revision book and discussed later in this Commentary concerns the 1966–1967 Commission's decision not to make substantive policy recommendations to the Convention's delegates (but to discuss issues, alternatives and the pros and cons of each alternative), I now note my experiences as counsel to government agencies that did make substantive policy recommendations:

(1) In my capacity as assistant counsel to the Joint Legislative Committee on Court Reorganization, I drafted the proposed Family Court Act. The draft was unanimously approved by the Democrats and Republicans on the Committee, whose Chairman was Daniel G. Albert, a Republican State Senator who went on to serve on the New York Supreme Court. The legislation was then unanimously approved by the Assembly (controlled by the Democrats), and by the Senate (controlled by the Republicans). I am proud that Jeremiah B. Bloom, a Democratic Senator who served as the Joint Legislative Committee's Secretary, speaking for the record on the floor of the Senate, commended me personally for my work on the Family Court Act.

(2) After I completed my service with the 1966–1967 Commission, I joined a law firm. At the urging of the senior partner of the firm, I later agreed, while continuing my private practice, to serve as the part-time Executive Director and Counsel of the Suffolk County Charter Revision Commission. The function of that Commission was to review the

Suffolk County Charter and report "recommendations with respect to the amendment or revision thereof." All of the Commission's recommendations, ranging from the creation of a new County Legislature to the pioneering adoption of an Environmental Bill of Rights, were approved by a Democratic County Executive and Republican Board of Supervisors. On recommendation of the Commission, its proposals (unlike those submitted in a single package by the 1967 Constitutional Convention) were submitted as separate propositions to the voters. Each was adopted by the voters counted separately on county, town and village levels on triple referenda in elections held in two consecutive years.

(3) My work with the Suffolk County Charter Revision Commission and my earlier work for the 1966–1967 Commission later resulted in my being engaged, on a part-time basis, as special counsel to the Home Rule Committee of the Temporary State Commission on the Powers of Local Government, Robert F. Wagner, Chairman. (Mr. Wagner, a delegate to the 1967 Constitutional Convention, presumably approved my appointment as special counsel to the Home Rule Committee based on his familiarity with my work for the 1966–1967 Commission, of which he was a member.) While the Committee was responsible for making recommendations, my function was to present impartial briefing papers that did not contain recommendations.

(4) Based on my earlier experiences, I was asked in 1972 to become Counsel to the Temporary State Commission to Revise the New York City Charter, Senator Roy N. Goodman, Chairman. The members of this Commission had been respectively appointed by Governor Rockefeller, Mayor John Lindsay, the leadership of the New York State Senate and Assembly, the then New York City Board of Estimate

and the New York City Council. After I had been interviewed personally by the Chairman, the Mayor and representatives of other appointing authorities, my appointment as Counsel was unanimously approved by the Commission, which later asked me also to serve as Executive Director. I insisted that staff and consultants in the first instance limit their reports to briefing papers without any recommendation on the principal policy issue facing the Commission: whether to propose the political decentralization of New York City. I explained that the staff function was to assist the Commissioners make informed judgments on important policy questions. (When the nine months I had agreed to serve came to an end, I left the Commission to return to private practice.)

C. *My Relations with Sol Neil Corbin*

As I make clear later in this Commentary, I fully agreed with the 1966–1967 Commission's unanimous positions in the Commission's reports that:

(1) The Commission *should* make specific recommendations for enactment by the Legislature of laws needed to support the Convention and for the adoption by the Convention of rules for the conduct of its important business, and

(2) The Commission should *not* attempt to make substantive policy recommendations on the constitutional issues facing the Convention delegates elected by the voters, but should provide them with a series of objective reports that analyzed issues, stated alternatives and presented in an impartial way the arguments for and against each alternative.

Knowing that Mr. Corbin had been counsel to the Republican Governor Rockefeller, I (a Democrat) especially admired his principled insistence that the 1966–1967 Commission and staff function in a nonpartisan way. Indeed, the Commission members also operated that way. For example, the Commission's unanimous recommendation for the adoption of a procedural Convention rule establishing a strong office of President of the Convention was based on persuasive historical precedents and was made after it became clear that Anthony J. Travia, the Democratic Speaker of the Assembly, would be elected President of the 1967 Convention.

As a result of my admiration for Mr. Corbin's performance as Commission Chairman, when years later my work with the New York City Charter Commission was coming to an end, I became his partner in the law firm then known as Corbin & Gordon. I remained his partner until about 1978, when I resigned to form the law firm of Lauer & Kessler. Until this year, Mr. Corbin and I had seen one another infrequently in the 20 years since that resignation and do not have any professional or political contacts.

3. Lauer's Commentary Correcting and Supplementing Dullea's Flawed Discussion of the Commission

As will become clear in the following pages, Mr. Dullea's discussion of the 1966-67 Commission suffers from his failure to follow a rudimentary research procedure: to conduct interviews with those who carried a major responsibility for the organization, operations and reports of the Commission and who might present facts to challenge the version of events that may have been presented to him by others who may have participated in or observed the process. As one of those Mr. Dullea did not interview, I now present in chronological order specific facts to correct and supplement the flawed discussion in Dullea's Book. The obvious starting point is his discussion of the conflict early in the Commission's history over the choice of an Executive Director.

A. *Conflict Over Choice of Executive Director*

As Mr. Dullea writes, the Commission at first consisted of 12 Democrats and six Republicans. When the Republicans gained control of the New York State Senate as a result of the November 1995 elections, this arrangement changed. Mr. Dullea writes (on page 132 of his Book) that the then Speaker of the Assembly, Anthony J. Travia, and the Majority Leader of the Senate, Earl Brydges, "had agreed in the end of March [1966] to continue the Commission with an equal number of Democrats and Republicans, but no appointments had been made." Mr. Dullea continues:

> "Armed with this reassurance and support from the Governor, [Henry T.] Heald [the Commission's Chairman] went ahead and announced the staff ap-

pointments of Dick Atkins as research director and Columbia Law School's Louis Lauer as counsel. Unfortunately, Heald had apparently failed to review his plans in detail with the legislative leaders, and no action was forthcoming on the appropriation.

"April turned into May and still no funds were available to pay the staff employed by Heald, and on June 1 he publicly allowed that he was considering resigning as a result of the 'intolerable situation' created by the lack of legislative cooperation." (Emphasis supplied.)

Here is the full story inadequately suggested by Mr. Dullea's remark that "unfortunately" Mr. Heald "had apparently failed to review his plans in detail with the legislative leaders":

At the conclusion of the Commission's meeting on April 1, 1966 (the first I attended as Counsel to the Commission), Mr. Heald asked me to come with him to his office, which I of course did. As he walked to his desk, he took an envelope out of his pocket and told me that it had been handed to him by Harold L. Fisher, a member of the Commission, who was also Counsel to Speaker Travia. Mr. Heald then told me that the letter confirmed that Speaker Travia had asked that Ralph A. Straetz, a Professor of Government at New York University, be appointed Executive Director.

Mr. Heald pointed out to me that he had already appointed Richard Atkins, Director of the New York State Office of Local Government, as the Commission's Director of Research and he was reluctant to appoint Straetz as Executive Director.

Having served as an assistant counsel to the Joint Legislative Committee on Court Reorganization (of which Mr. Travia had been an *ex-officio* member who attended committee meetings) and having had some experience with the legislative process, I immediately concluded that, if feasible, some way should be found to avoid a conflict between Mr. Heald, as Chairman of the 1966–1967 Commission, and Assembly Speaker Travia. So, I responded by observing to Mr. Heald that, depending on context, the term "counsel" is used to refer to a single lawyer or to two or more lawyers. Wouldn't it be possible, I asked Mr. Heald, to devise appropriate titles to permit Straetz and Atkins both to serve in senior positions, thus making room at the same time for his and for the Speaker's choices?

In response, Mr. Heald disclosed, in our first serious discussion since my appointment as Counsel, the full range of his objections to appointing Ralph Straetz as Executive Director — whether or not Atkins was continued in a senior position. He began by reminding me that he had been Chancellor of New York University before he moved to the Ford Foundation and had remained friendly with the person who had been head of the New York University Government Department in which Straetz was a professor. Mr. Heald continued that when Straetz had been informally recommended by Speaker Travia for appointment as Executive Director, Mr. Heald had "checked him out" with his friend, the former head of the NYU Government Department. Based on that conversation, Mr. Heald told me, he had decided that Straetz was not sufficiently qualified to be the Commission's Executive Director.

At this point, Mr. Heald also reminded me that he was determined to run a nonpartisan commission. He continued that it was, in his judgment, absolutely necessary to have senior staff whose loyalty ran solely to the Commission through him, as Chairman. Speaking with feeling, he then said that if he appointed Straetz as Executive Director because the Speaker had formally requested him to do so, Straetz's loyalty would run to the Speaker (rather than through the Chairman to the Commission) and he (Heald) would no longer be assured that the staff would function in a nonpartisan way. He therefore was unwilling to accept the compromise I had suggested.

B. *Impact of the Conflict over the Executive Directorship*

As Mr. Dullea writes — and as I, a then unpaid Counsel with a family to support, vividly remember — "April turned into May and still no funds were available to pay the staff employed by Heald". It seemed obvious at the time — and seems obvious some 30 years later — that the reason "no funds were available" is that Speaker Travia, not the "legislative leaders", was unwilling to permit an appropriation for the Commission to be approved by the Assembly so long as his choice for Executive Director, Ralph Straetz, was not appointed to that position. As Mr. Heald remained unyielding in refusing to make the appointment and the Speaker unyielding in refusing to make funds available without the appointment, the deadlock put in serious question whether the Commission would be able to carry out its preparatory work for the 1967 Convention delegates in a timely way.

As the deadlock continued, I became increasingly concerned that the Commission indeed would not have time to deal with the complex body of detailed rules and broad policies into which the New York State Constitution had evolved. When I discussed this concern with Mr. Heald, he encouraged me to recruit legal staff and told me that he had been assured that funds would ultimately be made available to pay salaries retroactively to the respective dates of employment. I then proceeded to recruit recent honor graduates of Columbia Law School to work with me. (As I recall, Mr. Atkins, who was uncertain about his continuation with the Commission, proceeded more slowly than I to recruit staff.)

In these circumstances, I considered what work my staff and I should undertake while the deadlock over the Commission's Executive Director continued. I concluded that whatever the Commission's ultimate agenda and orientation might be, the Commission and the Convention would benefit from an understanding of the State's constitutional history and the experience of earlier constitutional conventions. So, I undertook, with the legal staff, studies of the State's earlier constitutional conventions and the evolution of the Constitution the Convention delegates would be reviewing. I also began, with the assistance of my young staff, to line out substantive constitutional issues that the Commission and then the Convention might wish to consider. At the same time, the legal staff considered in the light of past experience what legislation might be needed to support the Convention and what rules the Convention might adopt for its organization and functions.

Searching my memory of those difficult days, I cannot state with certainty the extent to which I discussed these specific matters with Mr. Heald, although I have a distinct recollection of discussing my general plans with him for his approval. However, the absence of funding and the uncertainty surrounding Mr. Heald's position as Chairman for three months delayed the engagement of consultants and employment of more staff and thus the time at which the

Commission's reports were eventually submitted to the delegates to the Convention.

C. *The Deadlock is Broken*

Mr. Heald never told me of the discussions, if any, he had with the Governor, the Legislative Leaders or their representatives before he resigned as Chairman on June 27,1966. Nor did he discuss with me his plans to resign or the manner of his resignation. However, after his resignation, four actions became public:

(1) The membership of the Commission was changed from six Republicans and 12 Democrats to an equal number of Democrats and Republicans.

(2) Sol Neil Corbin, a member of the Commission,was designated the new Chairman, an unpaid position.

(3) Ralph Straetz was appointed Executive Director.

(4) The Legislature enacted a Supplemental Budget that contained a $650,000 lump-sum appropriation for the Commission in addition to the $150,000 initial appropriation that Mr. Heald had not been able to use fully.

The deadlock had been broken. (Soon after, I was delighted to receive a paycheck for my work from April 1 through June 1996 and learn that the other members of the Commission's staff had received their pay for their work from the date they had respectively been employed by the Commission through June 1996.)

D. *Relationship Between Mr. Corbin, Chairman, and Ralph Straetz, Executive Director*

Mr. Corbin was elected in early July 1966 as the new Chairman. (He had served as Counsel to Governor Nelson A. Rockefeller for several years, ending in 1965, when he returned to private law practice as a partner in a New York City law firm.) I recall that shortly after his appointment as Chairman, in his first meeting with Mr. Straetz and me, he said that when he had accepted the designation as Chairman, the Governor and the Legislative Leaders had agreed that he and his wife would not have to cancel a long-planned European vacation starting in late July. He then made it clear that he expected the staff to function in a nonpartisan way and asked Mr. Straetz, as the Executive Director, to prepare (in consultation with me) a proposed line-item budget and proposed research plan for Mr. Corbin to consider when he returned from vacation with a view to submitting them to the full Commission for approval.

When Mr. Corbin returned from vacation several weeks later, he asked Mr. Straetz in my presence if he had completed a proposed budget and research plan. The answer was negative. Mr. Corbin then reiterated his prior request to Mr. Straetz.

Many weeks continued to go by without my receiving from Mr. Straetz a draft budget and research plan for my comment as Counsel, and Mr. Corbin made it clear to Mr. Straetz that he had not received for his consideration any proposed budget and research plan. Finally, Mr. Corbin asked Professor Straetz and me to meet with him at the Commission offices about 10:00 a.m. on Saturday, September 17, 1966 to receive and discuss the proposed budget and research plan he had asked Mr. Straetz, as Executive Director, to prepare.

When I walked into the Commission's conference room shortly before 10:00 a.m. that Saturday, I still had not received a draft budget and research plan from Mr. Straetz for my comment. The lights were on. I saw Mr. Corbin seated alone at the conference table, but did not see Mr. Straetz. There were not any papers in view.

Mr. Corbin and I said our hellos. To my amazement, he then asked me whether I had heard of a news story about the Commission the day before. I answered that I had not. He then told me — and the memory of this startling news is as fresh as I write this as it was when he finished giving it to me — that he had been told that the news media reported that Ralph Straetz was resigning as Executive Director of the Commission, charging that it was riven by politics. Mr. Corbin continued that the report apparently did not refer to the Chairman or me and it did not mention that Mr. Straetz was to have delivered the following morning a proposed budget and research plan for discussion with the Commission's Chairman and Counsel. Mr. Corbin then said that he had never received a draft budget or research plan from Mr. Straetz, and asked if I had. I told him I hadn't.

I then asked Mr. Corbin whether Mr. Straetz had ever complained to him that the Commission was riven by politics or had ever threatened to resign. Mr. Corbin moved his head from side to side and answered, "Never."

E. *Mr. Dullea's Discussion of Straetz's Resignation*

Here is Mr. Dullea's discussion in his Book (at p. 134) of the Straetz resignation — followed by the facts as I know them:

> "Policy conflicts, exacerbated by personality clashes between Straetz and Louis Lauer, led to Straetz's resignation on September 19 amid public recriminations with Corbin. These setbacks were highly demoralizing to the staff...."

(1) *Personality clashes.* Mr. Dullea does not indicate the basis, if any, for his assertion that there were "personality clashes" between Mr. Straetz and me. If Mr. Dullea had communicated with me in any way about any aspect of the Commission, its staff, its work product or its objectives, I would have told him that I do not recall any "personality clash" with Mr. Straetz. I do recall that I and some of the bright young lawyers on my staff, who had worked side-by-side with me when staff was not being paid, were concerned that Mr. Straetz did not seem to have a clear understanding of (a) the content of the New York State Constitution, (b) the scope of the materials the delegates would require to make informed judgments at the Constitutional Convention and (c) the way the legal staff could work together with Mr. Straetz and his staff. (This may have led Dr. Kenneth D. Clark, a member of the Commission, to conclude, according to a September 21, 1996 article in *The New York Times*, that the trouble was "clearly the inability of the executive director to work with counsel, and visa versa.")

(2) *Policy conflicts.* As for the "policy conflicts" that Mr. Dullea asserts led Straetz to resign, Mr. Dullea explains (at p. 133):

> "Straetz, reflecting the orientation of the Democratic members (Fisher, Bergan, and Marshall), pressed hard for the endorsement of specific policy recommendations. Corbin, Moore and the other Republicans generally opposed this strategy, arguing instead that the Commission should limit its efforts to a review of alternatives — a posture somewhat at variance with their earlier stand on the Peck Commission."

Here, too, Mr. Dullea does not indicate the source of any of these statements. As he never communicated with me, I know that I am not. If he had, I would have transmitted the following information to him (in addition to information on the reasons for the Commission's orientation):

(a) *The imagined variance in posture.* As a simple comparison of the public reports of the Peck Commission and 1996-1997 Commission establishes, except for Francis Bergan, who served as Vice-Chairman of both Commissions, and Abraham D. Beame (also a Democrat), no member of the 1966-67 Commission had been a member of the Peck Commission. Specifically, Corbin and Moore and the other Republican members of the 1966-67 Commission had not been members of the Peck Commission. Thus, it cannot be accurately stated, as Mr. Dullea asserted, that the "posture" of Corbin, Moore and the other Republican members of the 1966-67 Commission was "somewhat at variance with their earlier stand on the Peck Commission" of which they had not been members.

(b) *Pressing for specific policy recommendations.* I have no recollection that Straetz "pressed hard for the endorsement of specific policy recommendations" to the 1997 Convention delegates. I do recall that soon after his appointment at Executive Director, he asked me for — and I gladly gave him — copies of all the research papers that had been prepared to that date by Counsel's office. Straetz never said to me then or at any other time that he was — and I never had the impression that Straetz was — "reflecting the orientation of the Democratic members (Fisher, Bergan and Marshall)" in any discussion we had.

I now note for the record my personal knowledge of the extent, if any, to which Harold Fisher, Judge Bergan and Burke Marshall manifested an "orientation" different from that followed by the Commission:

(i) *Harold Fisher.* I did not discuss with Harold Fisher privately whether the Commission should seek to make specific substantive policy recommendations to the 1997 Convention delegates or limit itself to identifying issues, presenting alternatives and setting forth the arguments for and against each alternative. Hence, I cannot of personal knowledge confirm whether or not Mr. Fisher in private discussions with others "pressed hard" for the Commission to make specific policy recommendations.

However, my recollection is that Mr. Fisher made only one objection during the Commission's consideration of the many matters touched in its two procedural and thirteen substantive reports. That objection concerned the Commission's Report 2, entitled "Toward an Effective Convention: Legislative and Other Recommendations" dealing with procedural, not substantive issues — and did not involve the

Commission's "orientation". Indeed, Mr. Fisher voted in favor of every recommendation made by the Commission in Report 2 and all the other Reports, but only voiced opposition to my recommendation to the Commission that Report 2 contain an appendix that set forth the texts of the statutes dealing with preparations for the earlier New York State constitutional conventions. As it had been difficult for Commission legal staff to find those legislative precedents, the other Commission members decided to include the text of the earlier legislation for the benefit of future preparatory commissions and constitutional conventions.

(ii) *Francis Bergan.* As an admirer of Judge Bergan's decisions on the New York Appellate Division and the Court of Appeals, I paid close attention to his views on the work of the Commission and was especially pleased to join him in presenting the Commission's plans to a meeting of the Special Committee on the Constitutional Convention of the Association of the Bar of the City of New York. I am certain that he did not state at that meeting that the Commission would — or should — make specific policy recommendations on any substantive constitutional issues. And I cannot recall a single instance in which he or any other Commission member disagreed with, or questioned, Mr. Corbin's ultimate vote that the Commission, in rendering its substantive reports to the elected delegates charged with the responsibility for decision, should limit those reports to a statement of issues, alternatives and the arguments for and against each alternative — leaving it to the elected delegates to make the policy decisions. I also am not aware of a single instance in which Judge Bergan "pressed hard for specific policy recommendations."

(iii) *Burke Marshall.* Mr. Marshall was no longer a member of the Commission when its reports were prepared, and I do not recall a single instance in which he "pressed" at any meeting of the Commission for the endorsement of specific policies. (He had resigned as a member of the Commission, as I recall, to take a position at Yale Law School, and had been replaced by Theodore C. Sorenson, former Counsel to Presidents John F. Kennedy and Lyndon Baines Johnson.) Before his resignation, however, Mr. Marshall, whose activities in the Kennedy Administration on behalf of civil rights I admired, and I spoke privately about the Commission. In those conversations, he did not "press" for, or even advocate, any specific policy recommendations on any substantive constitutional issue or urge that the Commission make recommendations on substantive constitutional issues.

F. *Facts Bearing on Straetz's Resignation*

In place of Mr. Dullea's glittering claim of "policy conflicts" and "personality clashes" to account for the Straetz resignation, I submit the following facts:

(1) Mr. Straetz, as Executive Director, never produced a proposed Commission budget and research plan for review by the Chairman, for comment by Counsel or for consideration by the Commission or any of its subcommittees.

(2) On the Saturday morning following the first public disclosure of his resignation, the Chairman told me that Straetz had never complained to him about the Commission's orientation or his relationship with me and had

never threatened to resign before he submitted his written resignation.

(3) I had — and have — no sense of "personality clashes" between me and Mr. Straetz, but do have a clear recollection of my inner concern about his apparent limited knowledge of the history and content of the New York Constitution and of the materials the Commission should prepare to assist the elected delegates perform their function.

(4) I never had any "policy conflicts" with Mr. Straetz.

(5) The contemplated resignation was disclosed to the news media the day before Mr. Straetz was to have met with the Chairman and me to present his proposed budget and research plan — and, according to the Chairman, without any prior notice from him to Mr. Corbin personally or to the Commission.

In view of these facts, I am deeply skeptical that Straetz resigned over "policy conflicts exacerbated by personality clashes" between Mr. Straetz and me, or the Chairman. Conceivably, he may not have liked the Chairman's long-standing request that Mr. Straetz, as Executive Director, produce a budget and program for consideration by the Commission, (which Mr. Straetz never did fulfill), but he never said so to me.

G. *Impact of Straetz's Resignation*

(1) *Public recriminations.* Mr. Dullea's states (at page 134), without providing or citing any supporting source or data, that "Straetz's resignation on September 21 [occurred] amid public recriminations with Corbin". I was puzzled

when I read that text because I did not recall any "public recriminations."

I was also curious about the absence of any supporting facts or citation in Mr. Dullea's book. So, I undertook quick research into *The New York Times*'s contemporaneous report in its September 21, 1966 issue (at p. 36). This disclosed that Howard J. Samuels, then Democratic candidate for Lieutenant Governor, Frank D. O'Connor, then Democratic candidate for Governor, and Franklin D. Roosevelt, Jr., then Liberal candidate for Governor, "assailed" Governor Rockefeller while Mr. Samuels separately called on Governor Rockefeller "to obtain the resignation" from the Commission of Mr. Corbin, former Lieutenant Governor Frank C. Moore, and Dr. William J. Ronan, Governor Rockefeller's Secretary and Chairman of the Metropolitan Transportation Authority. (Not mentioned in *The New York Times* article, Dr. Ronan had been Executive Director in 1958 of the Special Legislative Committee on the Revision and Simplification of the Constitution, Nelson A. Rockefeller, Chairman.)

Putting what Mr. Dullea calls "public recriminations" in context, *The New York Times* article continued that "Mr. Samuels drew a rebuff from Senator Jacob K. Javits, the Governor's [Rockefeller's] campaign chairman and head of the Republican slate for delegates-at-large to the 1967 convention." The article then quoted the "rebuff":

> "'Surely Mr. Samuels must be joking,' the Senator said. 'Frank Moore is acknowledged by responsible leaders in both political parties to be the state's outstanding expert on local government. Dr. Ronan has a long and distinguished record. Sol Corbin, as

counsel to the Governor, developed extensive expertise on the function of government."

At least according to this contemporaneous article in *The New York Times*, then, the "public recriminations" amid which Straetz's resignation occurred were harsh campaign criticisms by the Democratic candidate for Governor, the Democratic candidate for Lieutenant Governor and the Liberal candidate for Governor. This might suggest the possibility that the "recriminations" were purely political in nature — a possibility that a disinterested scholar would make certain to include in his report to enable a reader to make an informed judgment about the "public" reaction to the reported Straetz resignation.

Indeed, to enable readers to make an informed judgment concerning these so-called "public recriminations," a careful and disinterested scholar would have brought to the readers' attention the information contained in the following contemporaneous reports from *The New York Times*:

(a) In its December 20, 1965 issue (at p. 35), the newspaper had reported on the appointment of 18 "prominent New Yorkers," including former Lieutenant Governor Frank C. Moore, Dr. Ronan and Mr. Corbin, as Commission members "to map plans for the 1967 Constitutional Convention." It further reported that Howard J. Samuels (not then an announced candidate for Lieutenant Governor) praised the 18 appointments. Samuels "said," according to the Times, "he was delighted that nominations 'of such high caliber' had been made," declaring that the "most qualified and capable figures in the state should be encouraged to participate at every stage in preparation for and work in the Constitutional Convention."

(b) In its June 30, 1965 issue (at p. 27), the newspaper reported on a major mistake discovered in a bill proposing a code of ethics for state employees that led Senator Joseph Zaretzki, the Democratic majority leader, to postpone Senate action on the bill enacted by the Assembly. The Times report continued:

> "Mr. Zaretzki said the mistake was discovered by Sol Neil Corbin, Governor Rockefeller's counsel. 'And I always said the Governor was smart in getting himself a smart lawyer,' Mr. Zaretzki commented."

(2) *Demoralized staff.* Mr. Dullea's book also does not provide any source or facts to support the statement that Mr. Straetz's resignation was a "setback" that was "highly demoralizing to the staff." Based on my personal observations of "staff" in the days following Mr. Straetz's resignation and related press reports, it was obvious that different members of staff responded differently to the resignation, as follows:

(a) The members of staff recruited by Ralph Straetz during his two-and-a-half months as the Commission's Executive Director waited to see what would happen to them and the Commission. I do not recall that any Straetz-recruited staff left the Commission as a result of Mr. Straetz's resignation.

(b) The young lawyers on Counsel's staff were confident that they would continue with the Commission and looked forward to the appointment of a new Executive Director with more knowledge than Mr. Straetz had shown about the history and content of the New York State Constitution. Rather than being "demoralized", they were hopeful that a new Executive Director would facilitate preparations for the imminent constitutional convention.

(3) *Significance of the distorted presentation of the impact of Mr. Straetz's resignation.* The contrast between Mr. Dullea's unsupported statements about the Straetz resignation occurring amid "public recriminations" and "highly demoralized" staff, on the one hand, and the contemporaneous report of *The New York Times* and my clear recollections, on the other, are troubling in what purports to be a scholarly work. At the very least, that contrast suggests that Mr. Dullea's discussion of the circumstances surrounding Mr. Straetz's resignation and its effects either suffers from strangely inadequate research, or is simply a partisan account that exaggerates the impact of the Straetz resignation, or both.

Under the heading of inadequate research, I note that the book does not refer to the contemporaneous report in *The New York Times*, which would have alerted an objective analyst to the possibility that some candidates for public office were seeking attention by making unfounded charges. I also note again that Mr. Dullea failed to communicate in any way with Mr. Corbin (the person with whom, according to Mr. Dullea, Mr. Straetz had "policy conflicts") or with me (the person with whom, according to Mr. Dullea, Mr. Straetz had "personality clashes") in an effort to test whether Straetz's resignation was the result of "policy conflicts exacerbated by personality clashes." He also failed to communicate with me — the head of the legal staff and one remaining senior member of staff in a position to observe staff reactions — about the effects of the Straetz resignation on staff. Based on my own extensive research experience, I consider those failures "strange" even if Mr. Dullea would have chosen not to accept either Mr. Corbin's or my report.

H. *The Commission's Approach*

According to Mr. Dullea, the Commission was divided along political party lines on whether it should make "specific policy recommendations" or "limit its efforts to the review of alternatives". Without any documentation, he thus writes (at p. 134):

> "Less certain about the necessity for constitutional change, the Republicans wished to keep available as many options as possible."

It is at this point in his narrative that Mr. Dullea (1) states that Mr. Straetz resigned on September 21, 1966 because of "policy conflicts exacerbated by personality clashes", (2) reports that in mid-October the Governor, the Republican Majority Leader of the Senate and the Democratic Speaker of the Assembly agreed on the appointment of Dr. Robert S. Herman as the new executive director, and (3) continues:

> "*The selection of Herman*, a career public servant who had served in major positions in the Division of the Budget under both Harriman and Rockefeller and who was personally liked by both legislative leaders, *brought to an end the public conflict over the role of the Commission.* The Democrats acquiesced to the Republican preference for a listing of alternatives, and Herman was instructed to do his best in as workmanlike a fashion as possible in the remaining six months before the start of the Convention." (Emphasis supplied.)

I have no personal knowledge of the process by which Dr. Herman was selected as the new Executive Director or of the "instructions", if any, he was given. I therefore refrain from any comment on Mr. Dullea's statements about that process and those "instructions". I can, however, supplement from the public record and my personal recollections Mr. Dullea's version of how the Commission came to focus on substantive issues, alternatives and the presentation of arguments for and against each alternative, and not to make policy recommendations on substantive constitutional issues.

A convenient starting point is an editorial entitled "Constitutional Confusion" in the September 24, 1966 issue of *The New York Times*. Written within days after Mr. Straetz's resignation, the editorial remarked:

> "Since the delegates are being selected along partisan lines, the issues to come before the convention will of course be debated by the parties as such. But ideally the delegates should have the benefit of factual research which has been prepared in an impartial, nonpartisan way. That is why a distinguished figure from outside active politics — Dr. Henry T. Heald, former president of the Ford Foundation — was originally named chairman of the preparatory commission. But because the Democratic leadership in the Assembly insisted on naming the chief of staff, Dr. Heald eventually resigned."

Ten days later the Commission, under Corbin's chairmanship, began a previously planned series of four public hearings on "what portions of the Constitution should be retained, supplemented, simplified or eliminated" (to quote from the Commission's Report 1, "1967 Convention Issues: Introductory Report", p. 20). Held in Albany on October 3, in Buffalo on October 4 and in New York City on October 10 and 11, 1966, these hearings gave the Commission an added sense of the issues that seemed to concern active participants in public life.

On October 13, 1996, *The New York Times* reported (at p. 39) that Mr. Corbin had said after the hearings that "three major issues" were emerging for consideration at the 1967 Constitutional Convention: church-state relations, fiscal home rule for localities, and the selection of judges. The Times's article also reported that Mr. Corbin had "observed" that other issues "could attract more public interest before the convention opens in Albany next April". It then continued:

> "[Mr. Corbin] said that the commission had not decided yet whether it would make recommendations to the convention on proposed constitutional changes or confine its preparations to objective reports for the delegates with background information on pending issues and summaries of various viewpoints.
>
> "'There is some sentiment for making recommendations and some sentiment for not making them,' Mr. Corbin said."

As matters developed, the Commission completed its first report to the convention delegates on December 22, 1996, little more than two months after the completion of its public hearings. Entitled "1967 Convention Issues: Introductory Report," this report described (at. pp. 10-11) the

Commission's subject areas and the composition of its three subcommittees, and stated that the Commission "as a whole will have primary responsibility for the reports of Convention Organization and Procedures and on Constitutional Revision and Simplification." Unanimously adopted, the Introductory Report then formally stated the Commission's program (at. p. 11):

> "The Commission is examining the existing provisions of the Constitution, proposed changes and new constitutional concepts in the light of their purpose, their impact in practice and their relevance to the future. In its reports the Commission will strive as objectively as possible to present the issues, together with the alternative proposals for meeting them, the reasons for and against each proposal and the probable effects of each."[11]

Without dissent, the Commission also stated in this December 22, 1996 report (at p. 9) that in addition to those studies of constitutional issues, "the Commission will report to the Governor and the Legislature on legislation needed to prepare for an effective Convention." This report on necessary legislation, the Commission wrote, "will be submitted early in the 1967 session of the Legislature."

Keeping its word, on January 11, 1967, the Commission submitted to the Governor and the Legislature the Commission's unanimous Report 2, "Toward an Effective Conven-

---

11 This report was written after Theodore C. Sorenson had been appointed to the Commission to fill a vacancy caused by the resignation of Burke Marshall, and he joined all of the other members of the Commission in approving the report.

tion: Legislative and Other Recommendations." On February 12, 1997, it transmitted to the delegates to the Convention its unanimous Report 5, "For Effective Constitutional Review: Convention Organization and Rules."

The Commission's Reports 1 (the introductory report), 2 (on legislation required for the Convention) and 5 (on Convention organization and rules) reflect the Commission's practical sense of the difference between (1) legislation and procedural rules dealing with the functioning of the Constitutional Convention, on the one hand, and (2) resolution of substantive constitutional policy issues, on the other. Drawing on its study of the difficulties and successes of earlier conventions and on the substantial body of government experience shared by members of the Commission, the Commission's nine Democrats and nine Republicans resolved the relatively limited procedural issues involved in structuring the Convention. The references in Report 5 to historical precedents and to the similarities and differences between the Legislature and the Convention make this clear. Report 5 explains why, contrary to Mr. Dullea's sense of partisan divisions within the Commission after Mr. Corbin's appointment, the *Republicans joined with the Democrats* in the Commission's unanimous recommendation for strong executive leadership at the Convention — a recommendation made after the voters had given Democrats control of the Convention and thus when the entire Commission understood that a Democrat would be President of the Convention.

In contrast, constitutional issues involving local finance; the right to vote; education; the administration of criminal justice; state finance; housing, labor and natural resources; individual freedoms; welfare, health and mental health; the judiciary; local government; and state government — to list the titles of the Commission's 11 reports on substantive constitutional issues — concern a broad range of competing considerations. Those competing considerations involve what Justice Felix Frankfurter once called a difficult choice between competing "goods" (for example, should all Judges be elected or appointed and if so, by what process?), rather than a simple choice between a "good" and an "evil". In the Commission's judgment, such public policy choices between competing "goods" should be made by the elected Convention delegates and not the appointed commissioners.

I. *Initial Assessment of the Commission's Work and Staff*

Mr. Dullea reports (at p. 134) that "interviews with several members of the Convention's leadership lead me to conclude that the Commission's work and its staff were rapidly forgotten." His own discussion of the Convention's development of a proposed Bill of Rights (rather than my personal knowledge of the extent to which the Convention's leadership, the delegates to the Convention or their staffs were aware of and used the reports) casts doubt on the breezy statement that the Commission's work and its staff "were rapidly forgotten."

(1) *The Commission's work.* Although I have not read Mr. Dullea's entire book, I note that in discussing the Convention's work on a proposed Bill of Rights, Mr. Dullea discusses (at pages 253-56) the Convention debate over the issue of wiretapping and electronic eavesdropping. He begins that discussion with the following reference to the Commission's report analyzing the issue that contradicts his earlier conclusion (at p. 134) that the Commission's work and staff had been "rapidly forgotten":

> "The debate over proposed modifications of the existing constitutional guarantees concerning unreasonable searches and seizures mirrored the arguments set forth in the *comprehensive analysis* prepared by the Temporary State Commission on the Constitutional Convention [citing in footnote 7 the Commission's Report, "Individual Liberties: The Administration of Criminal Justice," pp. 39-114]. In *one of its most comprehensive submissions to the Convention*, the Temporary Commission outlined the fundamental problems of conflicting values that faced the delegates." (Emphasis supplied)

At this point in his book, Mr. Dullea quotes at length from the Commission's presentation of "the fundamental problems of conflicting values that faced the delegates" — hardly evidence that the work of the Commission was "rapidly forgotten".

(2) *The Commission's staff.* Mr. Dullea qualifies his statement that the Commission's staff was "rapidly forgotten" by referring (at p. 134, note 8) to a statement by Robert Herman, who had succeeded Professor Straetz as the Commission's Executive Director.

Significantly, Dr. Herman — head of the supposedly forgotten Commission staff — had been appointed Executive Assistant to the President of the Convention, Anthony J. Travia (in itself hardly evidence that the Commission's staff had been "rapidly forgotten"). According to Mr. Dullea, rather than confirming that the Commission's staff had been "rapidly forgotten," Mr. Herman told him "that other commitments of his senior staff precluded their participation in the Convention."

I can confirm the truth of Dr. Herman's statement in my own case. Having worked, as my wife put it, seven days and six nights a week during my tenure as Commission counsel, I had chosen to join a New York City law firm, effective immediately upon my completion of my work for the Commission, and was not available to serve on the Convention's staff even if asked to do so. In addition, as to others on the Commission's counsel staff, an assistant counsel was to become law clerk to a U.S. District Court Judge; another assistant counsel had accepted a law school faculty appointment; and several other assistant counsel (each of whom had an outstanding academic record) were to be associates in major New York City law firms. Those commitments precluded their participation in the Convention.

J. *Assessment of Commission Reports*

Of more practical significance for future preparatory commissions and constitutional conventions than Mr. Dullea's "rapidly forgotten" statement are the facts that seriously put in question the reliability of the following discussion by Mr. Dullea (at p. 134 of his Book) of the Commission's reports:

> "Donna Shalala has written that the Commission's thirteen substantive reports were 'non-controversial and uneven in quality' and that they did not appear to have been used widely by the Convention delegates, at least with respect to the urban issues principal to her concern. Interviews support this finding in all subject areas, though the lateness of the reports' completion was also a major factor in their underutilization. *Once the Democrats had won control of the Convention, the legislative leadership*

essentially ceased giving serious consideration to the Corbin Commission, and its chairman responded in kind." (Emphasis added.)

The documentary record establishes that the Democrats won control of the Convention at the general election held in New York State on November 9, 1996 — before any of the Commission's reports had been written. If true, Mr. Dullea's statement that the "legislative leadership essentially ceased giving serious consideration" to the Commission once the Democrats won control of the Convention would be a devastating comment on the preparatory process for the 1967 Convention. For it would strongly suggest that the "legislative leadership" never gave any "serious consideration" to any of the Commission's reports — all of which were written after the Democrats won control of the Convention.

Speaking accurately, after the 1996 general election, the "legislative leadership" included, among others, Earl W. Brydges, the Republican Majority Leader of the State Senate; Anthony J. Travia, the Democratic Speaker of the Senate; Joseph Zaretzki, the Democratic Minority Leader of the State Senate; and Perry B. Duryea, the Republican Minority Leader of the Assembly. As the Republican leaders and their staffs in Mr. Dullea's distorted version of events would presumably have had reason to consult the Commission reports, it seems almost certain the "the legislative leadership" — who, according to Mr. Dullea, never gave any serious consideration to the Commission — consisted of the Democratic leaders and their staffs.

The involvement of Harold L. Fisher, Counsel to Speaker Travia and a member of the Commission, raises serious questions even about that more restrained statement. I specifically recall Mr. Fisher's active participation in meetings of the Commission's Subcommittee on State Government, Legislative Apportionment, Suffrage and Methods of Constitutional Amendment (William J. Ronan, Chairman) and in meetings of the full Commission. I had assumed during those meetings — and, notwithstanding Mr. Dullea's statement, still assume — that Mr. Fisher kept Mr. Travia informed of the main thrust of the Commission's work.

Questions remain (a) whether the Commission's reports arrived too late to be used by the Convention leadership, delegates and staff, and (b) if they did not arrive too late to be used by the Convention leadership, delegates and staff, whether they were worthy of attention.

To put these questions in an objective context, I compiled, for each of the Commission's 16 reports, hard data on: (i) the date it was transmitted to the delegates and, in the report calling for legislation, the date it was transmitted to the Governor and legislative leaders; (ii) the number of pages in the report; and (ii) the number of outside consultants, if any, who participated in the report. Here is the resulting profile:

Statistical Profile of the Commission's 16 Reports

Report	Title	Date Transmitted	No. of Pages	No. of outside Consultants
1	1967 Convention Issues: Introductory Report	1/5/67	78	none
2	Toward an Effective Convention: Legislative & Other Recommendations	1/11/67	72	none

Statistical Profile of the Commission's 16 Reports				
Report	**Title**	**Date Transmitted**	**No. of Pages**	**No. of outside Consultants**
3	Local Finance	2/12/67	168	4
4	The Right to Vote	3/5/67	83	3
5	For Effective Constitutional Review: Convention Organization and Rules	3/13/67	48	7
6	Education	3/21/67	90	1*
7	Individual Liberties: The Administration of Criminal Justice	3/24/67	211	13**
8	State Finance	3/24/67	186	3
9	Housing, Labor, Natural Resources	3/24/67	119	4
10	Individual Freedoms	4/5/67	67	3
11	Welfare, Health and Mental Health	4/5/67	103	3
12	The Judiciary	4/5/67	292	16
13	Local Government	4/5/67	150	5
14	State Government	4/5/67	227	12
15	Revision and Simplification	4/5/67	35	none
16	Subject Index	4/5/67	48	1
ALL			1,977	75
* Academy for Educational Development, Inc.				
** Treating the National Council on Crime and Delinquency as one Consultant				

Before turning to the significant questions raised by Mr. Dullea's quoted paragraph concerning the Commission's reports, two preliminary observations are in order:

I compiled the data set forth in the table (the "Statistical Profile") from the Commission's 16 reports in little more than an hour and my secretary typed them in the grid in which they are presented in about an hour. The limited amount of time required to compile and type the data indicates that it was not the burden of compiling and presenting the data that accounts for their absence in Mr. Dullea's book.

The Commission as a whole worked on its introductory report (Report 1), its recommendations for legislation needed to support the Convention (Report 2), and its recommendations for rules to be adopted by the Convention to define its organization and operations (Report 5). All of the other reports (except for the subject index presented in Report 16) were first considered by a Subcommittee of the Commission and then acted on by the full Commission. The members of the respective Subcommittees brought to their respective areas of responsibility established expertise and known policy preferences.

Because the work of the Subcommittees helps in the appraisal of Ms. Shalala's comment quoted by Mr. Dullea, I note here some of the respective Subcommittee members and their obvious expertise. For example, Dr. Kenneth D. Clark, highly regarded for his work in Brown v. Board of Education, the landmark case decided by the United States Supreme Court, and other matters of public concern, was Chairman of the Subcommittee on the Bill of Rights and Social and Economic Policies. He was joined on that Subcommittee by, among others, Theodore C. Sorenson, former

Counsel to Presidents Kennedy and Johnson; Harold M. McNiece, Dean of St. Johns Law School; and Mrs. June Martin, a long-term State official. These members, among others, assured that the Commission reports on substantive issues involving the Bill of Rights, including church-state relations and discrimination based on race or gender, were focused and nonpartisan. They also assured that information relevant to the 1967 Convention delegates' consideration of social and economic policies embodied in the State Constitution was presented in Commission reports on those items.

Frank C. Moore, a former State Comptroller and Lieutenant Governor, and an acknowledged expert in local government, was Chairman of the Subcommittee on Public Finance and Local Government. Robert F. Wagner, another expert and former Mayor of New York City, was Vice-Chairman. They were joined by, among others, Abraham D. Beame, former Budget Director of New York City, who was later elected as Mayor of New York City, and Daniel J. Reidy, a local government official in Westchester County, also acknowledged experts. These Subcommittee members brought to the areas of their responsibility substantial experience in the workings of local government, the relationships between local and state government, the tensions involved in public finance and competing political considerations. With their colleagues, they helped assure that Commission reports in their areas of responsibility dealt with significant issues and were not tilted to favor any Democratic or Republican position, where those positions may have differed.

William J. Ronan, Secretary to Governor Rockefeller and former Dean of the NYU School of Public Administration, was Chairman of the Subcommittee on State Government, Legislative Apportionment, Suffrage and Methods of Constitutional Amendment. He was joined by Daniel Gutman, who had served as Counsel to Governor Harriman, by Harold L. Fisher, who (as I have noted earlier) was Counsel to the Speaker of the Assembly and by William Hughes Mulligan, Dean of Fordham Law School. They brought to their Subcommittee an awareness of the workings of state government, the relationships between the executive and legislative branches of government, sensitivity to the political dimensions of legislative apportionment and awareness of different methods of constitutional amendment. With their colleagues on this Subcommittee, they assured that the Commission reports in their areas of responsibility did not overlook practical considerations and were not tilted to favor one political party's position over the other.

With these observations and the Statistical Profile in mind, I now turn to the two significant questions raised by Mr. Dullea's quoted paragraph concerning the Commission's reports.

(1) *Were the Commission's reports timely?* The Commission and its staff were, of course, aware of the desirability of placing all of the Commission's reports in the hands of the delegates and their staffs before the delegates gathered in Convention in April 1966. At the same time, they understood that the delays in recruiting staff, engaging consultants and establishing the Commission's research program caused by the conflict between Mr. Heald and Speaker Travia made it extremely difficult to do so. The Statistical Profile indicates the extent to which the Commission was able to transmit its 16 reports before and shortly after the delegates convened.

Reflecting the Commission's priorities and the relative complexities of different constitutional issues, the respective transmission dates of the reports call for the following conclusions concerning the timeliness of different Commission reports:

(a) Reports 1 (convention experience and constitutional issues) and 2 (legislative recommendations to support the Convention) were transmitted by January 11, 1967 — in ample time for the delegates to begin reflecting on their work and for the Governor and Legislature to consider and act upon appropriate legislation for the Convention.

(b) Report 5 (Convention organization and rules) was transmitted on March 13, 1966. This provided sufficient time for the Convention delegates, leadership and staff to formulate appropriate rules and define the organization and procedures of the Convention.

(c) Report 3 (local finance) was transmitted on February 12, 1997. Consisting of some 168 pages, it was thus made in ample time for delegates and staff to study its contents and take them into account in planning and carrying out the Convention's work.

(d) Reports 4 (right to vote), 6 (education), 7 (individual liberties and the administration of criminal justice), 8 (state finance) and 9 (housing, labor and natural resources) were transmitted between March 5, 1967 and March 24, 1967 — all before the delegates gathered in Convention. In view of the magnitude of Reports 7 (211 pages), 8 (186 pages) and 9 (119 pages), it may be that those reports were not delivered in sufficient time to be used in the initial planning of Convention committee work. It seems highly probable, however, that those reports were made available in sufficient time to enable delegates and their staff to reconsider any initial plans and certainly to enable the delegates to test proposed constitutional changes in light of, as *The New York Times* September 24, 1996 editorial put it, "factual research which has been prepared in an impartial, nonpartisan way".

(e) Reports 10 (individual freedoms), 11 (welfare, health and mental health), 12 (judiciary), 13 (local government), and 14 (state government), each bearing an April 5, 1967 transmission date, were transmitted just after the Convention first met. Under the circumstances, it seems almost certain that they were not received in time to be used in the initial planning of committee work at the Convention. However, they were received in sufficient time to enable staff and delegates to review proposed constitutional changes in light of, "factual research which has been prepared in an impartial, nonpartisan way." Indeed, as noted above, Dullea admits that Report 10 was debated extensively at the Convention.

(f) The 35-page Report 15 (revision and simplification) bears an April 5, 1967 transmission date. Approximately 50% of this report consists of appendices that were respectively reprinted Chapter 1 of the 1959 Inter-Law School Committee Report, "The Problem of Simplification of the Constitution," and the 1961 final report of the Temporary Commission on the Revision and Simplification of the Constitution. In view of the complexities of the substantive constitutional issues discussed in the earlier Commission reports, the Commission focused in Report 15 on four alternative methods of simplification: an entirely new constitution; a two-part constitution with different methods of amendment; a constitution generally amended by referendum; and the transfer of technical specifications to statute law. On the assumption that the Convention would choose among these alternatives in light of its study of the existing constitution, the April 5, 1967 transmission date of Report 15 seems to have provided ample time for the study and possible use of this 35-page report.

(g) Report 16, the Commission's last report, consists of a 48 page index to the Commission's first 15 reports. Obviously, it could not be completed until the first 15 reports had been completed and either printed or in final page proof. While this resulted in the transmission of the index after the delegates had convened, it nevertheless was available to any staff member or delegate who wished to test a proposal against "factual research which has been prepared in an impartial, nonpartisan way."

(2) *Were the Commission's reports worthy of the attention of the Delegates and Convention Staff?* For clarity of analysis of the facts bearing on this question, I discuss separately the Commission's procedural and substantive reports.

(a) *Procedural Reports.* As I have already indicated, the Commission's unanimous Reports 2 (legislative recommendations) and 5 (convention organization and rules) dealt with specific procedural issues in light of New York's experience with earlier constitutional conventions and supporting legislation, and New York's legislative experience. The members of the Commission, Democrats and Republicans alike, were — I vividly recall — particularly pleased with these reports. I also recall the valuable assistance of the seven consultants the Commission had engaged to assist in the preparation of its report on Convention organization and rules. Among them were: Franklin Feldman, who had been Editor-in-Chief of the Columbia Law Review and who was at the time a partner in a major New York law firm; Howard N. Mantel, Esq., who had been my colleague on the Columbia University Legislative Drafting Research Fund and who was Counsel to the Institute of Public Administration when he served as a Commission consultant; and Leonard H. Sandler, Esq., whom I knew from my days as a member of the New York Young Democrats and who went on to become a State Supreme Court Justice.

(b) *Substantive Reports.* As the Statistical Profile shows, the substantive reports (all but Reports 1, 2, 5, 15 and 16) discussed a wide range of significant substantive constitutional issues in over 1,750 pages. Given the Commission's objective of providing impartial, nonpartisan briefing papers, it may be said that Donna Shalala's statement (quoted on page 134 of Mr. Dullea's book) that the Commission's substantive reports were "non-controversial" is a high compliment and evidences the extent to which the Commission achieved its objective.

This conclusion is confirmed — and a sense of the worthiness of the Commission substantive reports is strongly conveyed — by Mr. Dullea's discussion at pages 253-56 of his book, some 120 pages after he quotes Ms. Shalala. He there reports on the dramatic debate at the Convention about existing constitutional guarantees concerning unreasonable searches and seizure. Contrary to the impression he conveys in his discussion of the Commission on page 134, Mr. Dullea reports that (i) the Commission's "comprehensive submission" on unreasonable searches and seizures (Report 10, pages 39-114) outlined "the fundamental problems of conflicting values that faced the delegates", and (ii) the Convention debate "mirrored the arguments set forth" in the Commission's comprehensive analysis. It is a high praise, then, to say of a comprehensive report that outlines "fundamental problems of conflicting values" that it was, in Ms. Shalala's phrase, "non-controversial" — that is, neither side of the debate controverted the accuracy and fairness of the presentation of its views and of the opposing views.

Mr. Dullea also quotes Ms. Shalala's assertion that the substantive reports were "uneven in quality", but does not specify which of the substantive reports (each of which contained separate reports on specific issues within the broad category indicated by the report's title) were, in Ms. Shalala's opinion, of high quality, which of moderate quality and which, if any, were of low quality.

As Counsel to the Commission with a heavy responsibility for the preparation of the Commission's reports, I must leave to others a judgment as to the quality and usefulness of the respective reports. I may attest to the facts, however, that (1) the Commission Subcommittees and I made a special effort to select as consultants persons with established reputations in their respective fields, and (2) neither Mr. Heald, the Commission's first chairman, nor Mr. Corbin, the Commission's second chairman during whose tenure all of the Commission's 16 reports were written, recommended any patronage appointment or vetoed any of my choices for appointment to the Commission's legal staff or for engagement as a consultant.

On the assumption that a scholarly appraisal of the Commission's substantive reports would take into account the experiences and knowledge of the Commission members (discussed earlier in this Commentary) and the credentials of the Commission's consultants, I now discuss some of the consultants who contributed to two of the Commission's substantive reports on key issues that emerged from the Commission's public hearings.

Church-State relations (the "Blaine Amendment"). Determined to give the delegates to the Constitutional Convention a clear understanding of the limitations imposed by the United States Constitution on New York State's treatment of church-state relations, I engaged Robert B. McKay, then Dean of New York University Law School and an expert in constitutional law, to prepare a paper on this subject for Commission consideration. In accord with Commission policy, I made it clear to him that his function was to provide background information, an analysis of federal and the then state constitutional provisions on the subject, and to present objectively the issues, possible alternatives and the arguments for and against each alternative. His paper was substantially incorporated as part of the Commission's Report 10 ("Individual Freedoms"). As controversial as the Blaine Amendment was at the 1967 Convention, I never heard any criticism, public or otherwise, of Report 10 during or after the Convention.

Selection of judges. In an effort to assure that the Commission and, through the Commission, the delegates received a comprehensive, reliable and impartial report on methods of judicial selection (broadly, elective vs. appointive), I asked Robert Ensher to serve as the Commission's consultant on this sensitive issue. Mr. Ensher was a partner in what was in 1966 the small law firm of Skadden Arps. Some years earlier, we had been colleagues on the staff of the Temporary State Commission on the Courts, whose work had evolved into a revised Judiciary Article approved by the voters in 1961 and which would be reviewed by the Constitutional Convention in 1967. Mr. Ensher had an outstanding academic record, was not active in party politics and had the professional discipline required to satisfy the Commission's requirements for an objective briefing paper. Mr. Ensher's paper was supplemented by research done by the Commission's legal staff and was in large measure incorporated in the Commission's Report 12 ("The Judiciary").

Having considered methods of judicial selection as draftsman of the Family Court Act in 1962 for the Joint Legislative Committee on Court Reorganization, I was especially active in the preparation of this report. Judges of the Family Court within the City of New York are appointed by the Mayor; judges of the Family Court in counties outside the City of New York are elected by the voters. Unfortunately, the Commission did not have time to conduct an empirical, systematic study whether there was a significant qualitative difference between appointive and elective judges of this Court and, if there was, whether the difference related to the method of appointment or to differences in the roles of judges in New York City and in the suburban or rural counties outside of New York City. Without such an empirical, systematic study, I was especially demanding that the report on selection of judges submitted to the Commission for its consideration objectively present historical material, issues, alternatives and the arguments for and against each alternative. The resulting report was unanimously approved by the Commission members, including Judge Francis Bergan of the New York Court of Appeals.

K. *Mr. Corbin's Attitudes and Objectives*

I do not have any personal knowledge of the process by which Mr. Corbin was initially appointed a member of the Commission nor of the process by which he was appointed Chairman after Mr. Heald's resignation. Using the passive voice, Mr. Dullea simply states that "Sol Corbin was named the new chairman" and does not indicate who appointed him and whether (as I had speculated in July 1966) he had been elected as a result of agreement of Governor Rockefeller, Speaker Travia and Majority Leader Brydges. I do have personal knowledge, however, of Mr. Corbin's attitudes and objectives as they were manifested in my presence during his 9-month tenure as Commission Chairman. I now present that information to correct and supplement Mr. Dullea's discussion in Chapter 5 of his book.

1. *Attitude towards Mr. Straetz's appointment as Executive Director.*

Mr. Dullea writes (on page 133):

> "The Speaker had been given the right to select the executive director, and Sol Corbin was sorely distressed that the executive director of 'his' commission would be Ralph Straetz."

He does not provide or cite any facts to support the assertion that the Speaker "had been given the right to select the executive director"; that Mr. Corbin was "distressed" by what Mr. Dullea treats as the Speaker's appointment of Ralph Straetz; or that Mr. Corbin viewed the Commission as "his". I can state without hesitation that (a) Mr. Corbin never stated or demonstrated in my presence that he was "distressed" or "sorely disappointed" or unhappy with the Straetz appointment, as distinguished from Mr. Straetz's lack of performance as Executive Director, and (b) he never stated and never implied by word or by action that he considered the Commission "his".

On the contrary, until Mr. Corbin learned from the news media that Mr. Straetz had resigned, he continued in his discussions with me to assume that Mr. Straetz would produce the proposed budget and research plan he had asked for and would continue as Executive Director. And he invariably referred to the Commission either as "the Commission" or as "our Commission". In my experience (and, to judge from contemporary reports in *The New York Times*, in public discussions), until the Commission voted on an issue, Mr. Corbin was careful to avoid any statement suggesting that his personal views were the Commission's views.

2. *Attitude on selection of staff and consultants.*

I have discussed earlier in this Commentary the shoddy error in Mr. Dullea's statement (on page 133) that Mr. Corbin's position that the Commission should not make recommendations on substantive constitutional issue was "at variance with [his] earlier stand on the Peck Commission" — of which he had *not* been a member. I have also discussed in some detail the Commission's decision to limit its substantive reports to a discussion of issues, alternatives and the arguments for and against each alternative. As *The New York Times* editorial board understood, the reason for that policy was to assure that the delegates — of varied training and experiences — would have objective, factual and informative reports to use in resolving the difficult issues before them.

Mr. Corbin's attitude towards the selection of staff and consultants, as manifested in his instructions to me, reflected his determination to have the Commission produce such objective, factual and informative reports. He made it clear that the legal staff and consultants were to be chosen based on their professional competence, without regard to their political affiliations, and he never asked me to clear my selections with him. He also never asked me to appoint any staff member or any consultant based on political affiliation, and I was never asked by any party official, Republican or Democrat, to make a single appointment to staff or engage a single consultant.

I state without qualification that I strictly applied Mr. Corbin's instructions (which accorded with my deeply held beliefs) on the principle to be used in selecting staff and consultants. The obvious test of the accuracy of this statement, to which I would cheerfully submit, would be a review of the credentials and subsequent careers of the Commission's assistant counsel and the consultants I retained.

3. *Alleged ambition to become Counsel to the Convention President.*

Among the more amazing statements in Mr. Dullea's discussion of the Commission is the following (at page 134) concerning Mr. Corbin's motivation:

> "The [Democratic] outcome of the election [of delegates to the Convention] had eliminated Corbin's chance to become Counsel to the President of the Convention, thus wiping out any real interest on

his part in using the Commission to shape an agenda for the Convention and to educate the public on the possibilities for constitutional revision."

Mr. Dullea does not provide, and does not cite, *any* facts or sources to support (a) his assumption that Mr. Corbin *wished* to become Counsel to the President of the Convention; (b) his presumption that if Mr. Corbin had that ambition, he would have deemed it appropriate to use the Commission "to shape an agenda for the Convention," rather than provide the delegates with objective, factual reports for them to use in resolving difficult substantive constitutional issues; (c) his tacit assumption that the Commission members, all knowledgeable and experienced, would have tolerated an effort to "shape the agenda"; and (d) that the Commission's hearings and substantive reports did not help the public become aware of the possibilities — and the difficulties — of constitutional revision.

Contrary to Mr. Dullea's unsupported statement, I can state that *before the election* of delegates in which the Democrats won control of the Convention, — no less than after their election — Mr. Corbin never indicated in my presence, directly or indirectly, the slightest interest or desire in becoming Counsel to the President of the Convention. Significantly, it was before the election of delegates that Mr. Corbin gave me his instructions on the selection of legal staff and consultants and stressed his determination that the Commission function in a nonpartisan way. If, as Mr. Dullea implies without any scholarly foundation, Mr. Corbin had hoped to become Counsel to a Republican President of the Convention, and if, as Mr. Dullea implies, Mr. Corbin would have been willing to use the Commission "to shape an agenda" that would have advanced that assumed ambition, Mr. Corbin would either have replaced me (a Democrat) as Counsel with a deserving Republican or would have used his authority as Chairman to select staff and consultants to fashion the desired agenda. As I have already reported from personal knowledge and as the listed assistant counsel and consultants show, he did none of that *before or after* the Democrats won control of the Convention.

4. *Some Concluding Observations*

Having spent much of my life in academic research and in government service, it is clear to me that Mr. Dullea's discussion of the 1966-67 Commission in Chapter 5 of his Book is not based on appropriate research standards and does not adequately address basic issues of importance in planning for any future constitutional convention in New York State. Because of the gravity of my conclusions, I now focus the remainder of this Commentary on three aspects of Mr. Dullea's treatment of the Commission:

(1) The respects in which his research methods were inadequate;

(2) The respects in which his discussion of a three-month deadlock over the choice of the Commission's Executive Director failed to address what was at stake, and

(3) The respects in which his discussion of whether the Commission should have made recommendations on substantive constitutional issues fails to deal with the merits of the question and with the possible impact on the Commission of the 1965 election that gave the Demo-

crats control of the New York State Assembly and the Republicans control of the New York State Senate.

I also discuss the lesson to be learned from the 1967 Convention's decision to submit its 38 recommendations in a single package in an "all or nothing" basis.

A. *Inadequate Research Methods*

This commentary has noted on several occasions that Mr. Dullea did not interview Mr. Corbin, Commission Chairman during the period that all of the Commission's public hearings were held and all of the Commission's reports were prepared. Nor did Mr. Dullea interview me, Counsel to the Commission from its early history during the tenure of Mr. Heald, its first Chairman, through the transmittal of the Commission's last report during Mr. Corbin's tenure. Nothing in his book states that he sought, but was unable, to interview us. As neither Mr. Corbin nor I disappeared from public view and each of us openly and continuously maintained law offices in New York City in the 30 years from the Convention through the completion of Dullea's Book, it is highly unlikely that Mr. Dullea's failure to interview us was the result of his inability to locate either or both of us.

An obvious example of the consequences of that failure is the error contained in Mr. Dullea's suggestion that Mr. Corbin and other Republican members of the 1966-67 Commission had been members of the earlier (1959-1961) Temporary State Commission on the Revision and Simplification of the Constitution (the "Peck Commission"). A simple comparison of the lists of commissioners contained in the first pages of the published reports of the two commissions would have shown that not one Republican member of the 1966-67 Commission had been a member of the Peck Commission. Alternatively, a simple telephone call to Mr. Corbin or to me would have led Mr. Dullea to the reports (if, conceivably, he had not known of their existence) that would have shown him that not one Republican member of the 1966-67 Commission had been a member of the Peck Commission.

On a personal note, those facts drove me to consider what might have led Mr. Dullea, as author of what facially purports to be a scholarly work, mistakenly to assert — without any documentation — that "Corbin, Moore and the other Republicans generally opposed [having the 1966-67 Commission endorse] specific policy recommendations .... a posture somewhat at variance with their earlier stand on the Peck Commission," *of which they had not been members.*

The most plausible hypothesis to account for Mr. Dullea's failure to undertake the easy research that would have protected him from error is that, having prejudged the issue, it never occurred to him that research on this point was necessary. On this hypothesis, Mr. Dullea simply made the unscholarly assumptions that (1) all Republicans, whether named "Corbin" and "Moore" (who served on the 1966-67 Commission) or "Peck" and "Brydges" (who served on the 1959-61 Commission), were alike in their thoughts, actions and motivations, (2) they would act in an identical way (without regard to changes in circumstance or function), and (3) none would oppose in 1966 the endorsement of policy recommendations some Peck commission members favored in 1959-61. On this hypothesis, Mr. Dullea therefore did not feel under any obligation to research whether Republicans Corbin and Moore actually were on the Peck Commission and had changed their position or to inquire as to the reasons that led them, unlike members of the 1959-61 Peck Commission, to join their colleagues on the 1966-67 Commission in preparing substantive reports that were non-partisan briefing papers.

B. *Inadequate Exploration of Deadlock Over Choice of Executive Director*

Mr. Dullea's discussion of the three-month deadlock over the appointment of a Commission Executive Director also reflects a sad combination of inadequate research and prejudgments that resulted in a one-sided presentation of a critical event in the Commission's history.

During that three-month period (April, May and June 1966), the Commission was without clear direction from Mr. Heald, its Chairman, whose continuation in office had become progressively difficult and uncertain. It was without an Executive Director to prepare a line-item budget and help develop a research plan for Commission consideration. It was without funds to employ a full staff and engage needed outside consultants. And, under the circumstances, it was unable to generate public hearings and public interest in the substantive issues likely to be considered at the forthcoming constitutional convention.

These consequences of the three-month deadlock radiated throughout the nine months that remained from the date the deadlock was broken (by Mr. Heald's resignation, Mr. Corbin's designation as the new Chairman and the appointment of Speaker Travia's choice for Executive Director) to the date the delegates gathered in Convention. While I and the few assistant counsel I had recruited managed during the deadlock period to research New York's constitutional history and prior constitutional conventions and work at identifying issues that the delegates would be considering, our product was a fraction of what would have been accomplished during that three-month period by a fully-funded, fully-staffed Commission free from the deadlock. As a result, the Commission was under constant pressure to do in nine months what would have been difficult enough to accomplish in twelve months.

The three-month deadlock also impaired the Commission — and perhaps the Convention itself — in a more subtle way. As the days turned into weeks and the weeks into months, the deadlock seemed to create and then reinforce a false public impression of a Commission subjected to internal, rather than external, partisan wrangling. The deadlock thus made it most difficult for the public and the media to accept the Commission as a trustworthy agency effectively preparing for a Convention the voters had approved.

Against this background, the inadequacy of Mr. Dullea's exploration of the deadlock over the choice of an Executive Director is stunning. As I have noted earlier in this Commentary, Mr. Dullea first reported that Mr. Heald had appointed Dick Atkins as research director "and Columbia Law School's Louis Lauer as counsel". He then blandly continued with the following explanatory comment bearing on the deadlock:

> "Unfortunately, Heald had apparently failed to review his plans in detail with the legislative leaders, and no action was forthcoming on the appropriation."

As The New York Times September 24, 1966 editorial and other knowledgeable people understood, Mr. Dullea's unnamed "legislative leaders" were really one person, Anthony J. Travia, Speaker of the Assembly, who refused to permit the Assembly to enact the appropriation needed to fund the Commission as long as Mr. Heald refused to appoint Ralph Straetz, the Speaker's choice, as Commission Executive Director. And Mr. Dullea's statement — "Unfortunately, Heald had apparently failed to review his plans in detail with the legislative leaders" — to explain why "no action was forthcoming on the appropriation" can only be interpreted as a most indirect way of saying, "As long as Heald refused to appoint the Speaker's choice as Executive Director, the Speaker wouldn't fund the Commission."

At this point, two obvious questions — neither of which is explored in the Dullea Book — arise. Why didn't Mr. Heald take steps to correct what Mr. Dullea characterizes as an "unfortunate" failure "to review his plans in detail with the legislative leaders" by simply reviewing his plans with Speaker Travia after Harold Fisher delivered the Speaker's letter to him on April 1, 1966? And why didn't the Speaker permit the Assembly to enact the appropriation needed for the Commission to proceed with the preparatory work while discussions were had concerning the appointment of an Executive Director?

One conceivable answer to both questions is that the character of the individuals involved — Chairman Heald and Speaker Travia — compelled each stubbornly to seek to have his own way, without regard to the public consequences of his unyielding position. On this dubious theory (given their public careers), nothing more was at stake in the conflict over the choice of Executive Director than which of two obstinate men would prevail.

A second — and more likely — possible answer is that the conflict over the choice of Executive Director was in reality a conflict over the proposed Commission's orientation and program. This possibility takes into account that the Commission theoretically had at least the following four alternative ways of orienting its work:

(1) It could attempt to formulate a Democratic substantive program of constitutional revision.

(2) It could attempt to formulate a Republican substantive program of constitutional revision.

(3) It could attempt to formulate a bipartisan substantive program of constitutional revision.

(4) It could attempt to prepare impartial reports that defined issues, alternative solutions and the arguments for and against each alternative, leaving it to the elected Convention delegates to formulate or negotiate substantive constitutional programs for the electorate to adopt.

With these alternatives in view, it may be said that the conflict between Chairman Heald and Speaker Travia over the choice of Executive Director was a conflict over which of these alternatives the Commission would adopt.

On the one side, Mr. Heald was determined to have the Commission prepare impartial reports and, it may be inferred, was concerned that the Speaker, through his choice of Executive Director, would instead have had the Commission formulate a substantive program for the Convention satisfactory to the Speaker and his political allies in the Democratic party. On the other side, Speaker Travia may have been concerned that Mr. Heald, who had been appointed by Governor Rockefeller, would not be satisfied with impartial reports, but would in the end see that the Commission tilted its reports in favor of Republican positions. Alternatively, Speaker Travia may have concluded that Mr. Heald would produce impartial reports, and may have been unwilling to settle for reports that did not contain a set of substantive constitutional policies satisfactory to Speaker Travia and his allies.

If this theory (which is consistent with Mr. Dullea's references to Democrats "pressing hard" for the endorsement of policy recommendations), is correct, what can be made of Mr. Dullea's statement, "Unfortunately, Heald had apparently failed to review his plans in detail with the legislative leaders"? It could not simply mean that it was "unfortunate" that Mr. Heald did not, as a courtesy, "review" his plans in detail with the legislative leaders — leaving the unstated implication that if he had, his showing of deference would have led the "legislative leaders" to acquiesce in his choice of Executive Director and Commission orientation and enact the necessary budget appropriation. Nor, based on the facts presented in Chapter 5, did the quoted statement mean that it was "unfortunate" that Mr. Heald did not "review" his plans in detail with the legislative leaders, with the implication that if he had, he and Speaker Travia would have reached agreement, leading to the necessary appropriation.

Given what was at stake in the choice of Executive Director, Mr. Dullea's statement probably was intended to mean that it was "unfortunate" that Mr. Heald failed to *accept* Speaker Travia's choice of Executive Director and the Speaker's position on what the Commission's orientation should be.[12] Thus, the seemingly bland statement that it was "unfortunate" that Mr. Heald failed to "review" his plans in detail with the "legislative leaders" implies — without explanation or analysis — that Mr. Heald rather than the Speaker was (or both Mr. Heald and the Speaker were) responsible for the deadlock.

By omitting a candid discussion of what led to the deadlock and who was (or were) responsible for it, Mr. Dullea missed an opportunity to derive from the 1966 experience the insights that could prove useful in preparing for a subsequent constitutional convention. Because such insights require an exploration of both the Commission's ultimate decision to present impartial reports and the impact on the Commission of the results of the November 1965 election of State Senators and Assemblymen, I now explore those matters.

C. *Inadequate Discussion of the Commission's Orientation and the Impact of the 1965 Legislative Elections*

As presented in Mr. Dullea book, the Commission had two alternatives in deciding on what he refers to as its "orientation": (1) the Commission could set out to endorse specific policy recommendations for changes in the Constitution, or (2) the Commission could set out to present impartial statements of issues, alternative solutions and arguments for and against each alternative, without endorsing any specific substantive policy recommendations. These

12 Otherwise, Mr. Dullea would have written (1) that it was "unfortunate" that the Speaker did not accept Mr. Heald's choice of Executive Director and Commission program, or (2) that it was "unfortunate" that the Speaker was so insistent on his choice of Executive Director and Commission orientation that he withheld funds from the Commission.

choices were present when the Commission — formed in December 1965 during the administration of the Republican Governor Rockefeller when the Democrats controlled both houses of the New York State Legislature — consisted of 12 Democrats and 6 Republicans.

As matters developed, Mr. Heald felt compelled to appoint senior staff *after* the voters gave the Republicans control of the New York State Senate and continued the Democrats' control of the New York State Assembly, but *before* the November *1966* election of delegates that determined whether Democrats or Republicans would control the Convention. (If he had deferred the choice of senior staff until the outcome of the November 1966 election was known, the Commission would have had less than five months — obviously not enough time — to prepare reports on legislation and rules required for the Convention and on substantive constitutional issues to be considered at that Convention that began in April 1967.)

In short, the deadlock over the choice of Executive Director and Commission orientation developed at a time (1) when the number of Democrats on the Commission was about to be reduced from 12 (two-thirds of the Commissioners) to nine, a number that would deny the Democrats (even if they chose to vote as a block) control of the Commission, and (2) when no one knew for certain whether the Democrats or the Republicans would control the Convention through the election of delegates in November 1996. The Democratic Assembly Speaker's only chance to control the Commission's choice of Executive Director and orientation thus was to do so before the number of Democrats on the Commission was reduced. One may therefore infer that this reality led Speaker Travia to negotiate an agreement with the Republican Governor Rockefeller and Republican Senate Majority Leader Brydges, providing for (1) an equal number of Democratic and Republican Commissioners (rather than six appointed by each of the Governor, Senator Brydges and the Speaker), and (2) the designation of an agreed-upon Chairman and Executive Director before the Speaker would give his necessary approval to the appropriation of funds needed by the Commission.

Not having any personal knowledge of the relevant discussions among the Governor, Senator Brydges and Speaker Travia, I cannot assert with certainty that inference is correct. However, the documented facts that funds were appropriated at the time that nine Democrats and nine Republicans were members of the Commission, Mr. Corbin was designated Chairman and Mr. Straetz was appointed Executive Director tend to confirm the correctness of the inference.

On this analysis, the inadequacy of Mr. Dullea's discussion of a conflict over whether the Commission should press for substantive policy recommendations is overwhelming. There is no evidence that Speaker Travia or any other Democrat argued that the Commission should, as a matter of principle, endorse substantive policies even if he disapproved of them. Indeed, it seems clear that Speaker Travia was prepared not to fund the Commission rather than run the risk that the Commission would make substantive recommendations of which he disapproved.

In light of these facts, it is clear that when Mr. Dullea wrote of Democratic members of the Commission pressing for the endorsement of substantive policies, his book did not express the actual issue of "orientation" faced by the Commission. As no one on the Commission pressed for the endorsement in the abstract of substantive policy recommendations, the issue was whether the Commission should (1) endorse Democratic or Republican substantive policies, (2) attempt to negotiate bipartisan policy recommendations or (3) prepare briefing reports that defined substantive policy issues, presented alternative solutions and discussed the arguments for and against each alternative. The members of Commission, faced with these practical choices, and the knowledge that only nine months remained before the delegates gathered in Convention, *unanimously* decided that rather than be forced to engage in time-consuming partisan arguments, they would fulfill their responsibilities by providing the elected delegates with reliable research on which the delegates could develop or assess substantive policies.

This unanimous Commission decision casts a strange light on the three-month deadlock over the choice of Commission Executive Director. If Speaker Travia had been willing to accept such a decision from the outset rather than, according to Mr. Dullea's account, acquiesce in it when Robert S. Herman was appointed Executive Director in October 1996, the Commission might have been spared the deadlock. In any event, with the benefit of hindsight (and without knowledge of the other matters claiming the Governor's and legislative leaders' attention in 1966), it may be said that the ultimate compromise should have been effected earlier.

It may also be said that if Mr. Dullea had not been predisposed to present a one-sided view of what caused the deadlock, his book could have been an excellent vehicle for assisting those responsible for structuring future constitutional conventions in New York to avoid a recurrence of the kind of deadlock that impacted on preparations for the 1967 Constitutional Convention.

D. *"All or Nothing" or "Pick and Choose"?*

As reported in Dullea's Charter Revision, the 1967 New York State Constitutional Convention voted on September 26, 1967 to submit its 38 recommended changes in the New York Constitution to the State voters in a single package, on an all-or-nothing basis. Weeks later, on Election Day November 1967, the voters chose "nothing," rejecting the entire package by a margin of almost 3 to 1.

Those events occurred during the formative period of the 1967-70 Suffolk County Charter Revision Commission, which had been created to review the Suffolk County Charter and report "recommendations with respect to the amendment or revision thereof" to the Suffolk County Board of Supervisors. One of the Suffolk Commission members (Frederic Block) had been Chief Counsel to the Education Committee of the 1967 Convention; another (Bernard L. Burton) had been a delegate to that Convention and Vice-Chairman of its Committee on Bill of Rights and Suffrage. Sensing that the fate of their efforts might be determined by whether the Suffolk Commission submitted, as did the 1967 Convention, all of its proposals in a single package on an all-or-nothing basis, the 17 members of the Suffolk Commission carefully followed the public discussion for and against that form of submission.

When the Suffolk Commissioners learned of the November 1967 result, their first inclination was to draw a simple lesson from the bitter defeat experienced by the 1967 Convention: if they wished to avoid complete rejection of their efforts, they should avoid the Convention's all-or-nothing approach and, instead, give the voters a clear opportunity to pick and choose among the proposals for changing the Suffolk Charter. However, it was not until July 31, 1969 — some 21 months later — that their first inclination, tested by experience, ripened into a final recommendation that their proposed changes be submitted to the voters in separate propositions rather than in a single package.

By then, the Suffolk Commissioners had reviewed detailed staff and consultant reports; held preliminary public hearings; voted on numerous issues involving the County Legislature, the County Executive, county budgeting and capital programming; considered and voted on draft charter laws prepared by counsel to embody the Commission's decisions in those areas; prepared reports that discussed their recommendations (setting forth in appendices the text of proposed charter laws); held public hearings on those recommendations and proposed charter laws; and voted on each change in their recommendations requested by witnesses at their hearings. Only then did they decide to recommend that the Suffolk County Board of Supervisors submit the Commission's 1969 proposals in two groupings respectively concerning (1) the county budget and capital program, and (2) the County Legislature and the County Executive, rather than on an all-or-nothing single package. (The following year, the Suffolk Commission completed its work by recommending charter laws containing a new Environmental Bill of Rights and a revised Planning Article for the Suffolk Charter — both of which were enacted by the Board of Supervisors and approved by the Suffolk voters on triple referendum.)

The Suffolk Commission's unanimous August 1969 Report, *For Public Referendum: Two Charter Laws*, explained as follows (at pages 7-8) the Commission's 1969 decision:

> "There are points at which different parts of a charter come together in such a way that a change in one part necessarily produces a change in other parts. This finding has led some persons to argue in favor of submitting 'in one package' all of the proposals for revising a charter.
>
> "In urging that our recommendations on the Legislature, Executive and Budget be submitted to the voters in November 1969, the Commission has rejected the 'one package' approach. Having begun by reviewing the charter as a whole, we soon found it extremely useful to focus on specific issues—deferring for the time being our consideration of others. Our introductory report and our reports on the budget process and on the Legislature and Executive evidence the workings of this approach.
>
> "The public hearings held by the Commission convinced us of the rightness of this approach. Those who testified were able to focus on specific proposals and advance reasons for or against them—without bringing in the entire charter or even referring to another part of the charter. The theory advanced in support of the 'one package ' approach was thus contradicted both by our own experience and, more importantly, by three productive public hearings.

> "We rely on those experiences in recommending that the charter proposal we have made be grouped into two separate charter laws: one on the county budget and capital program, the other on the County Legislator and County Executive."

Elaborating, the Commission remarked on "how naturally budget items come together — and at the same time are separate from other items." It also quoted from its earlier report "that any serious review of the Legislative Article involved questions concerning the office of the County Executive and the practical relationships between the Legislature and the Executive." At the same time, the Suffolk Commission recommended

> "against any further separation of [the two] charter proposals into more propositions. Here, the issues are so closely related they should be presented to the voters and decided in a single proposition."

The Suffolk County Board of Supervisors agreed not to submit the Commission's proposals in a single package. However, it did not agree to submit only two questions to the voters. Instead, it presented as a separate question for referendum the most controversial recommendation made by the Commission. Contained in the revised Legislative Article proposed by the Commission, that recommendation involved the transformation of Suffolk's historic Board of Supervisors into a County Legislature — itself a source of controversy generated by the United States Supreme Court's one man, one vote decision. The recommendation provided (1) that the members of the new Legislature be elected from districts (rather than serve by reason of their election to the office of Town Supervisor), and — most controversial of all — (2) that a person be barred from serving at the same time as a local officer and a County Legislator.

Unlike the Charter Commission, the outgoing Board of Supervisors determined to make it possible for the voters on triple referendum to be able to choose to vote *for* a new County Legislature, but *against* prohibiting a local officer from serving at the same time as a county legislator. And so the Board decided to submit the following third question to the Suffolk County voters in 1969:

> "Shall a charter law containing the recommendation of the Suffolk ...Commission providing that mayors of villages, supervisors of towns and members of legislative bodies of towns and villages shall not be eligible to serve as members of the County Legislature [and] declaring that such rule may be altered only upon mandatory referendum...be approved?"

Given the choice, the voters on triple referendum answered this third question in the same way as they answered the other questions presented on recommendation of the Suffolk Commission: "YES".

It would be a misleading to conclude that *all* of the Suffolk Commission's charter proposals were adopted by the voters on triple referendum *solely* because they were submitted in separate propositions (in contrast to the rejected all-or-nothing single package submitted to the New York State voters by the 1967 Constitutional Convention). Other considerations almost certainly led to that result.

First, the Suffolk Commission reviewed the Suffolk Charter as Suffolk County was being transformed from "a rural county with stable responsibilities" to "a large county subject to massive population pressures and rapid change". Suffolk County Charter Commission, "A Blueprint for County Budgeting and Capital Programming," p. 8 (February 28, 1969). Hence, the Commission concluded — and set out to persuade many institutions and agencies in the formation of public opinion — that significant changes in government structure, budgeting, capital programming, planning and environmental protections were needed to meet the County's new situation. The day-to-day awareness of change in the County helped persuade others that significant changes indeed were required.

Second, the 17 member Commission consisted of five members appointed by the Democratic County Executive, five appointed by the Republican Presiding Officer of the County Board of Supervisors and seven appointed jointly by those officers. Among the seven joint appointees was Claire Sauer, who had for four years headed the Suffolk County League of Women Voters and who was unanimously elected by the Commission to be its Chair. Fully aware of the political affiliations of the Commissioners, Mrs. Sauer was determined to run a nonpartisan Commission. (As Commission Counsel and Executive Director, I strongly supported her determination, having made clear before my selection that I believed the Commission should function that way.)

As a result, the Commission set out from its earliest days to demonstrate by its action (1) that the Commission, with due regard for competing views, had fairly and openly considered what changes in Suffolk's government were required to meet the changes in the County's circumstances; and (2) that the Commission's proposals (formed within the limits imposed and opportunities provided by state and federal law) could therefore be approved with some degree of confidence that they would result in some improvements in the way Suffolk County dealt with its new circumstances.

To earn the required trust and confidence, the Suffolk Commission from the beginning insisted that staff and consultants function in a nonpartisan manner, defining issues, presenting alternatives and advancing arguments for and against the alternatives. It met with county officials. It made available to government officials and interested citizens copies of all staff memoranda and consultant reports. It held hearings before reaching conclusions. It then issued reports that included the text (with explanatory comments) of each charter law tentatively approved by the Commission; held hearings on those proposed laws; reviewed and formally voted, after discussion, on each change requested at those hearings; and then issued reports explaining what the Commission had done.

The memory of the overwhelming rejection by the voters of the 1967 Convention's all-or-nothing package continued to influence the Commission as it proceeded to make "a detailed study of the Suffolk County Charter and report of its recommendations with respect to the amendment or revision thereof." Respectful of the voters who would decide the fate of the Commission's work on a triple referendum (county, town and village votes being counted separately), the Commission voted in favor of separate pick-and-choose propositions rather than a single all-or-nothing package. For this reason, too, the Commission readily accepted the Board of Supervisors' decision to add a third question (whether local officials could at the same time serve as county legislators) to the two questions the Commission recommended be separately submitted to the voters.

Without the benefit of a controlled experiment or of systematic comparative studies, it would be imprudent in the circumstances I have described to assert that the work of the 1967-70 Suffolk County Charter Revision Commission would have suffered the same fate as the work of the 1967 Constitutional Convention if it too had submitted a single all-or-nothing package to the voters.

On the other hand, in the world of practical affairs, one is often required to draw inferences and to act without the benefit of controlled experiments or systematic comparative studies. And so I conclude with the benefit of some 30 years' hindsight (as I had earlier concluded when the Suffolk Commission acted) that in the absence of some "crisis" requiring exceptional action, voters should be given an opportunity to vote separately for constitutional changes they favor and against constitutional changes they disfavor rather than being confronted with single package on an all-or-nothing basis.

Appendix

Sol Neil Corbin
Biographical Information

Sol Neil Corbin is engaged in the practice of banking, corporate and securities law at Corbin Silverman & Sanseverino LLP, a New York City firm he organized over nineteen years ago. He was Counsel to the Governor of New York (Nelson A. Rockefeller) from July 1962 until September 1965 and Special Counsel to the Vice President of the United States (Nelson A. Rockefeller) from February to June 1975.

Mr. Corbin is a graduate of Columbia University (B.S., 1948) and Harvard Law School (J.D., cum laude, 1951).

In his last year of law school, he was recruited by Lawrence E. Walsh (later U.S. District Court Judge, Deputy Attorney General of the U.S. and Independent Counsel for Iran/Contra Matters) as an assistant counsel to the New York Public Service Commission, serving from 1951 until 1953. From 1953 until 1954, he joined Judge Walsh at the newly-created Waterfront Commission of New York Harbor, where Mr. Corbin was an assistant counsel and helped prepare the legal briefs sustaining the constitutionality of the bi-state statute.

Recommended by Judge Walsh, Mr. Corbin served as law clerk to Justice Charles D. Breitel, then of the Appellate Division, First Department, of the New York Supreme Court (later Chief Judge of the New York Court of Appeals), from 1954 to 1956. In 1956, he entered private practice of law in New York City.

On recommendation of Judge Breitel, Mr. Corbin joined the staff of the Counsel to Governor Rockefeller, serving first as assistant counsel beginning in January 1959 and then as first assistant counsel until July 1961, when he returned to private law practice as partner in a New York City law firm. When Governor Rockefeller's Counsel resigned in 1962 to return to private law practice, the Governor asked Mr. Corbin to return to State service as his Counsel. Mr. Corbin became Counsel to the Governor in July 1962, serving until September 1965, when he returned to private law practice.

While in private law practice, Mr. Corbin was appointed in January 1966 by Professor George W. Taylor, Chairman of the Governor's special Panel on Pubic Employee Relations, to serve as Counsel to the Panel. The Panel was appointed to develop legislative proposals to protect the public against disruption of vital public services by illegal strikes while, at the same time, protecting the rights of public employees. In three months, the Panel conducted its studies, rendered its public report and made landmark legislative recommendations, which were enacted into law at the legislative session in 1966.

From July 1966 to 1967, Mr. Corbin was Chairman of the New York State Commission on the Constitutional Convention. From 1970 to 1973, he served as a member of the

New York State Commission on the Powers of Local Government, chaired by Robert F. Wagner, former Mayor of New York City. From 1974 to 1975, he served as Chairman of the New York State Crime Control Planning Board.

In February 1975, Mr. Corbin was asked by Vice President Rockefeller to become his Special Counsel to assist him in connection with his Chairmanship of the President's Commission on CIA Activities Within the United States. The Commission was directed by the President to determine whether any CIA domestic activities exceeded the CIA's statutory authority and to make appropriate recommendations. Mr. Corbin served as Special Counsel until June 1975, when the Commission rendered its report of its findings, conclusions and 29 recommendations.

Mr. Corbin was a member of the New York State Banking Board from 1969 to 1976. From 1974 until 1990, he served as United States Trustee in Bankruptcy of Franklin New York Corporation, the holding company of Franklin National Bank, as a result of the largest bank failure in United States history. From 1992 until the present time, he has been counsel to the Trustee appointed by the Federal Court to liquidate the assets of banks formerly controlled illegally by the Bank of Credit and Commerce International (popularly known as "BCCI"), a rogue foreign bank.

In 1973, Mr. Corbin was appointed by Chief Judge Charles D. Breitel to an eight-member special committee to recruit the first administrator of New York State's court system. From 1988 to 1990 he served as a member of Chief Judge Wachtler's Committee to Improve the Availability of Legal Services.

For many years beginning in 1967, Mr. Corbin served as Chairman of the Commercial Law Subcommittee of the American Arbitration Association. He also has been a Trustee of The New York Public Library since 1977.

Mr. Corbin is a member of the American Bar Association, the Association of the Bar of the City of New York, the New York County Lawyers' Association (member, TriBar Committee on Legal Opinions, 1978-) and the American Law Institute. He is included in *Who's Who in America* and *Who's Who in American Law*.

April 6, 1999

Index

D

K

L

M

N